The Tragedy of Common Sense

JOHN P. CLARK

with an introduction
by Salvatore Engel-DiMauro

and a foreword by Ariel Salleh

Changing Suns Press
Regina, Saskatchewan
2016

The Tragedy of Common Sense
Copyright © John P. Clark
Introduction: Exposing Common Nonsense
Copyright © Salvatore Engel-DiMauro
foreword
Copyright © Ariel Salleh
This edition Changing Suns Press, 2016

Garrett Hardin, Living on a lifeboat, Bioscience, 1974, 24(10), 561-568
by permission of Oxford University Press

ISBN: 978-0-9951551-2-1

Cover image by Chris Kortright

Changing Suns Press
2138 McIntyre Street
Regina, SK
S4P 2R7 Canada
info@changingsunspress.com

http://www.changingsunspress.com/

Printed in Canada

Table of Contents

Foreword
by Ariel Salleh v
Introduction: Exposing Common Nonsense
by Salvatore Engel-DiMauro ix
Acknowledgements xix

Part I: The Power of Myth 4
We Hold These Falsehoods To Be Self-Evident 6
The Power of Abstraction 10
The Scandal of Particularity 12
The Ship of Foolishness 15
Hardin's Ratchet Job 18
Hardin's People Problem 22
The Myth of Carrying Capacity 26

Part II: From Ideology to Historical Reality 38
On Not Giving A Man A Fish 38
On Letting Indians Die 43
Looking To India 50
Hardin's Sinking Ship 55
Following the Common 59

Living on a Lifeboat by Garrett Hardin 70

Appendix: Global Fertility Rates (2014) 96

Bibliography 100

Foreword
by Ariel Salleh

    This small book will nourish people who care for the future of life on earth. John Clark's signature call is to build freedom and justice through mutuality—and for several decades, he has brought this grounded life-affirming politics to the environmental movement. As a teacher of philosophy at Loyola University, New Orleans, his writing has embraced anarchist thought, social ecology, ethics, dialectical reason, and mysticism. As an activist, he has given himself to educational innovation, green politics, hands-on community conservation projects, and the self-determination struggles of Papuan and Tibetan peoples. It was inevitable that Clark's compassion and intellectual integrity would eventually draw him to confront Garret Hardin's brutal notion of social engineering.

    If the year 1968 belonged to voices of liberation, the publication of Hardin's famous article "The Tragedy of the Commons" pulled the other way. His political claim was that global ecological degradation is a result of high reproduction rates among the poor. By his Malthusian reckoning, demographic increase and food availability are interdependent variables, so the simplest strategy for population control would be for nations like the USA to stop food aid to poor countries. Besides, Hardin argued, by helping irresponsible others, affluent societies compromise their own wellbeing—best to keep these masses off "the lifeboat." Based on this contradictory blend of mechanistic systems thinking and elitist Social Darwinism, Hardin's environmental advocacy became a self-righteous triage.

When adequately researched, the matter turns out to be precisely the reverse of Hardin's perception. In Clark's words: "industrialized societies that support their growth heavily through enormous per capita consumption ... exceed ... carrying capacity much more than poorer societies that consume little of such resources per capita" (p. 18-19). The biologist Hardin was clearly not aware that his would-be scientific thesis was framed by North American exceptionalism. Clark's elegant, often satirical essay exposes this bias, its factual inaccuracies, and logical errors. Working across disciplines and conceptual levels, his refutation is an exemplar for the critique of contemporary neoliberalisms—like the corporate-government-UN agency "green economy" introduced at Rio+20 Earth Summit.

Clark opens *The Tragedy of Common Sense* with a brilliant *tutorial on political ideology*. It is essential that thoughtful citizens learn how everyday common sense is often a mythical reversal of actual conditions, one that lets powerful people deny their manipulation of others by projecting blame onto them. In Hardin's text, this dynamic is reinforced by his mocking use of the term "guilt-addict"—just in case any reader is uncomfortable with his policy. This is where the philosopher's interest in dialectical reason comes in. For Clark, and other leading scholars of ideology critique, the popular concept will always be found to contain its opposite meaning. Thus Clark reveals the unexamined plausibility structure of Hardin's case to be firmly embedded in a visceral defense of the capitalist economy.

Beyond this, the book lays bare *the limits of reductionist methodology*. Hardin's narrow focus on demography and food overlooks the complex historical interplay of global business penetration, maldevelopment, and loss of local livelihood economies. His population graphs and algebraic indices may look like science, but smart arithmetic will never be accurate if it does not name and measure the right things. Again, the naive determinism of Hardin's population "ratchet effect" is contradicted by his judgment of the poor as lacking moral "fibre." Clark's scrutiny of international records shows no consistent correlation between demographic increase and food. And it is now known that ecologically benign organic farming could support an even larger world population than exists today.[1]

Clark's text is also, in part, a treatise on the *imperial way of living* and how transnational productivism cannot function without class, race, and sex-gender exploitation. The said material dependency of poor nations is a lie, in reality. It is affluent societies who depend on the natural resources and cheap labour of the geopolitical periphery. For every 1 kilo of product consumed by the global North, 5 kilos of living nature are extracted from someone else's habitat. This should be acknowledged as a "neocolonial debt" owed to communities of the global South after the enclosure of their means of subsistence for mining, forestry, or ill conceived climate policies like the Clean Development Mechanism. Hardin's racist diminishment of darker peoples is a denial of his own cultural complicity in this theft.

Similarly, *The Tragedy of Common Sense* can be read as an *affirmation of ecological feminist arguments* for eco-sufficiency and global justice. Just as capitalism cannot function without racism, so it cannot function without sexism and the often violent enforcement of women's unpaid domestic labours. The global economy is subsidised by these reproductive contributions—biological, economic, social, and cultural—and this labour extraction constitutes a massive unspoken "embodied debt" to women. Blaming "reproductive" women for environmental damage is an ideological surrogate for this domination. And Hardin's right wing Malthusianism can be found on the Left as well—from deep ecologists like Arne Naess to degrowth enthusiasts like Joan Martinez-Alier.

Clark's deconstruction of Hardin is timely, and it helps clarify *the current international refugee crisis* brought on by oil wars and corporate land grabs, banking scandals and free trade deals. The affluent neoliberal world's gross "ecological footprint" is leading to the greatest transcontinental displacement of populations known in history. It is hard to read Hardin's "lifeboat ethics" without thinking of these people, fleeing the Middle East, North Africa, and South Asia—many sent to drown with their children in the open sea. The plight of poor Central Americans crossing into the USA is a parallel case. If Hardin were still with us, would he demand an end to the military aid that devastates migrant homelands? What would he say on the global speculation in food commodities, dumped to keep prices high?

Finally, John Clark has written an overture to *the commons as a model of sustainability* based on a rational humanity-nature metabolism. Hardin's belief in private property, his ideological blindness to its inherent scarcity, competitive individualism, and alienation, deformed his understanding of "the commons", and turned his arguments into nonsense. Commoning is as much about humans living in reciprocity as it is about nurturing natural resources. A generation later, Hardin's "poor" give global environmental leadership with the principle of food sovereignty. As they say: "*Vivir bien* is neither wealth nor poverty. It's not waste nor shortage, nor deficiency nor luxury, but a life in harmony with all other beings, a type of coexistence that is intercultural, intergenerational and inter-biotic."[2]

Notes

1. Badgley, C. et al. 2007. "Organic agriculture and the global food supply," *Renewable Agriculture and Food Systems*, 22(1) 86–108.

2. Josef Estermann cited by Pablo Solon. 2014. "Notes for the Debate: Vivir Bien / Buen Vivir?," Systemic Alternatives: www.systemicalternatives.com.

Introduction: Exposing Common Nonsense
by Salvatore Engel-DiMauro

It was not long ago widely accepted or held as self-evident truth, in Western European polities, that the Sun revolves about the Earth or that drilling a hole in the head (trephination) would relieve migraines. More recently, democracy meant the exclusive participation of propertied white men, that whites were believed superior and women inferior to men, and North America was seen as land that whites deserve to conquer. There were and still are many other such beliefs now presumably, at least, less overtly stated, if not less common. These received notions are examples of what is otherwise known as common sense. Such ideas have been imposed on those suffering from oppression and violence through a combination of overt coercion and socialization processes in which the oppressed internalize aspects of the ideology that justifies their oppression. It took decades to centuries of struggle and even war to change society (including those communities negatively affected by common sense views) in such a way as to convince most that such self-evident truths have been self-serving lies or self-delusions.

What is meant here by common sense is a set of predominant ideas or assumptions about how the world is. They are ideas shared by most people in a society, so they need not be debated or discussed. Leprechauns exist because they do and everybody in their right mind knows that they do. In fact, such commonly and dearly held truths can bring on ridicule, marginalisation, or even violent reaction (think of what can happen in this society to those claiming that profit is an elaborate form of theft or that there are more than two sexes, or think about what will happen to you if you deny the existence of leprechauns!). One major tenet in countries like the United States is that private property has always existed and, to some, it is part of human nature. A corollary to this is the belief that the best (if not only) way to manage resources properly is by individuals owning them (this, importantly, implies having a government or some coercive force protecting owners from people who might want to take their property). Another core belief is that people's situation reflects their individual choices in life and/or moral character. The rich deserve to be so because they made the right decisions in life and/or are morally superior.

Garrett Hardin (1915-2003), a microbiologist and ecologist, was among the most vociferous upholders of these two self-evident truths in the scientific establishment. His notions of "tragedy of the commons" and "lifeboat ethics", introduced between the late 1960s and early 1970s, became instant hits, spreading far and wide like a most persistent poison ivy that only grows more robust with each mowing. To summarise, the more famous of Hardin's arguments, "the tragedy of the commons," is that sharing is suicidal. In fact, one must be vigilant against "the evil of the commons" (Hardin 1968, 1248). Only private property and "mutual coercion" leads to responsible use of resources. Freedom to breed (bear in mind that his spouse had four children with him) is especially bad because it leads to pollution, resource depletion, and all sorts of environmental destruction, that is, to him the "tragedy of the commons." Hardin reckoned that "The fundamental error of the sharing ethics is that it leads to the tragedy of the commons" (Hardin 1974, 174). This grand thesis was therefore intimately tied to his subsequent pronouncement that there is a limit to how many people can live and it is due to carrying capacity or lifeboat size. Those who have access to resources (who live in the rich lifeboats) should not bother trying to re-distribute resources because carrying capacity will only be exceeded and everyone will suffer. Carrying capacity refers to the maximum population of a species that an area's resources can sustain indefinitely without being depleted or degraded. The argument is focused especial-ly on food and Hardin deems food aid as hindering the balance (i.e., large numbers of dead by starvation) that otherwise would be restored when population contracts to levels sustainable by the carrying capacity of an area (he takes country boundaries as the areas). Sharing is not only awful for the environment, but it is collectively ruin-ous (Hardin, 1974, 172-173).

These two arguments are quite closely aligned with common sense notions that private property is to be taken for granted as the way things have always been and that people more or less deserve their lot in life, especially if they dare live beyond their means (e.g., carrying capac-ity or lifeboat size). There are not a few fatal flaws with these arguments and most are discussed in John Clark's fine-grained analysis below. I would only like to point out some of the problems here that complement Clark's thor-ough take-down of Hardin's theses. One is that it is fasci-nating that Hardin's litany of truisms were published in major scientific outlets (*Science, BioScience*) in spite of his work contravening the most basic of conventional scien-tific standards. In his "tragedy of the commons" article, there is no evidence ever supplied to support the claims and no analyses are offered of any actually existing com-mon property systems. Moreover, Hardin confused the commons with what are considered open-access resourc-es and he conveniently failed to mention any of the abun-dant examples of environmental devastation brought about with private and state property systems. Similarly, Hardin's lifeboat ethics piece offers virtually no supporting evidence, while the demographic evidence he used can only prove his point if most of the rest of the data are ignored. Furthermore, the lifeboat metaphor is baseless because applying the concept of carrying capacity on people is outright silly. It is amazing how it could be lost on Hardin and the editors of such influential scientific journals that people have scarcely ever relied on resources in one area, especially with all the worldwide trading in myriad resources from all over the planet already by the 1800s. The concept does not even work for migratory species, especially bird populations flying about multiple places thousands of kilometres from each other (see also Sayre 2008). So much for scientific ecological thinking.

But Hardin's tragic argumentation turns runny on its own mouldy foundations. In his "tragedy of the commons" story, he asks us to "[p]icture a pasture open to all," where herders bring their cattle at will, ending up collectively destroying the pasture through overgrazing (Hardin 1968, 1244). In his "lifeboat ethics" melodrama, where we are confronted with either looking out for ourselves or helping others at our own peril, he wants us to pretend that rich people are so because they are on large lifeboats (greater carrying capacity) and the poor one are so because they live in small lifeboats (lower carrying capacity).

One should pause to reflect on these story lines for a bit. Thinking it through (something one should not do with common sense arguments!), it seems the cattle being brought by the herders bringing about "the tragedy of the commons" are not actually cattle that are "open to all." They are presumably owned by the herders. What is more, the herders apparently never speak to each other. They each furtively take the cattle to pasture and cleverly hide from the rest of the herders. So, rather than having anything to do with the commons, the tragedy would appear to be about privately owned cattle and the inability or unwillingness of the herders to communicate with each other.

Mulling over the story that carrying capacity is like a lifeboat, there is something that does not quite compute. The lifeboats are presumably floating on a sea and if so then the seas also have food resources, like algae, fish, and other edible marine life forms. Not only that, smaller boats could be more agile and effective in facilitating people gathering food from many different areas of the sea than bulkier, possibly slower boats. Who needs a huge lifeboat when there are abundant food sources all around? The population could easily remain stable relative to carrying capacity, which in reality greatly exceeds the lifeboat size. Still, Hardin is right about the possibility of having so many people in smaller lifeboats such that they will easily capsize. Yet what is unclear is where people on the differently sized lifeboats got the materials to build the lifeboats in the first place. Maybe the people in the larger lifeboats stole the materials from the people that are now in the smaller lifeboats! In the next chapters, John Clark will investigate this very issue further, even if somewhat differently.

Reasoning through common sense narratives and looking for data that support or contradict those stories can help build some intellectual immunisation from facile argumentation and, arguably, make for credible science. What is effective about common sense narratives is that one need not inspect whether an illustrative parable is logical according to its own assumptions. Actually, one better refrain from doing so at the risk of finding out that the assumptions are self-contradictory from the start. For it must be self-evident, in the case of the "pasture open to all," that it is impossible to share a resource without communicating about it and agreeing to how it will be used and distributed among those sharing it. Hardin must really have been referring to private owners who think they can take resources at will, which is not really sharing, now is it? Unfortunately, he could not recognise this little big hole in the story line, nor can those who mechanically repeat the story to this day. This is because they all take it as common sense that private property is good and communal property is, in Hardin's very words, "evil."

It must be underlined that both of Hardin's publications incurred criticisms from other scientists in subsequent issues of the same journal, but these have been to no avail. Thousands of academic manuscripts have been published that take, "the tragedy of the commons" as scientifically sound and even as a starting point of analysis into all sorts of research topics, ranging from the exploitation of worker bees by larvae among *Melipona* stingless bees (Wenseleers and Ratnieks 2004) to plant roots' alleged competition over soil nutrients (Semchenko, Hutchings, and John 2007). The commons can be virtually anything and anyone and even bee larvae are seen as a bunch of exploiters of worker bees that have the aim of becoming queens. Those nasty, self-centred larva! Disconcertingly, in terms of much wider reach, most textbooks addressing environmental issues include uncritical rehashing of Hardin's tragedy parable, such as a most recent one published for high-school level environmental science (Friedland and Relyea 2015, 331-332).

Common sense arguments in academic settings are hardly confined to conventional scientific or education institutions. They pop up almost anywhere, like mindless proverbs. While at a temporary job involving the marking of thousands of environmental science exams in the late spring of 2015, I overheard co-workers talking about the distribution of snacks that were placed in a common table and how they were fast disappearing because people were taking them at will. One of them quipped how this snack consumption problem was a classic demonstration of the "tragedy of the commons." A few weeks earlier, at a conference on self-managed housing and workplaces, during a session on the division of work in collectively run workplaces, a colleague traced the problems of effective coordination in rotating work responsibilities to the "tragedy of the commons." I could expect my temporary job co-worker and environmental scientist to be conversant with and readily invoke this argument, but not my colleague at the conference, given that person's anti-establishment views. Another colleague and I quickly intervened to let it be known that the concept of "tragedy of the commons" says actually nothing about the commons, but more about common sense assumptions prevailing in some parts of the world like Western Europe and North America.

These two experiences reveal how socially pervasive and persistent certain untenable notions become and how important it is to keep exposing their fallacious and pernicious nature. The repetition of Hardin's baseless claims in scientific publications and in everyday conversations has impacts on what kind of policies are formulated and applied for environmental conservation. It is one way in which authoritarian measures can be justified regarding, for example, the distribution of drinking water, using the excuse that, to avoid water resource depletion, limits must be enforced on water use regardless of who actually consumes what amounts and for what purpose. It is usually the poor who suffer most from the consequences of such measures. The implications of Hardin's arguments for government policies are also devastating for many communities that hold land and other resources in common. Impositions of private property regimes, especially on Indigenous Peoples, have been all too frequent. They have tended to reduce resource access for those communities and to benefit large corporations with handsome profit margins, and often with environmentally devastating effects. In the overwhelming majority of cases, land *has not been degraded* under communal management, but has been under private and public ownership or when communal management is undermined, as by colonial or national state authorities (Ostrom 1990; Ricoveri 2013; Roberts and Emel 1992; Wall 2014). It will be a major step forward in environmental conservation when it will become common sense that communal property regimes tend to encourage resource conservation. But it will take much struggle to change society so that current common sense assumptions about private property and individual responsibility are overturned.

Even the most illogical and empirically groundless ideas can have great traction and diffuse like wildfire when they cohere with widely held beliefs (common sense) and especially with those of the powerful. This alone should be enough reason to try to identify what passes as common sense and then take it apart to see whether it makes any sense. One can start by being skeptical of ideas that resonate readily with what we think is true and by doing research on what is known about the related topics. Reading this book is one way of getting acquainted with how to uncover and take apart common sense arguments, specifically about environmental problems. It is not easy to spot common sense notions and then it is even tougher to take them apart. To some extent, it can be difficult because we might be attached to those ideas, and anyway going against the grain is not really much fun, socially. But it is possible to overcome these problems and John Clark shows us the way brilliantly in this volume, exposing the nonsense in common sense. Doing this is worthwhile (and it can even be amusing) because it helps clear our heads of confused concepts and see through arguments used to justify the unjustifiable, like stealing resources and blaming the victims of that theft for not having enough resources.

As a final musing, here is a first step towards

overcoming this tragedy of common sense by correcting Hardin's own words (Hardin 1968, 1244):

> The tragedy of capitalist society develops in this way. Picture a shared pasture. It is to be expected that each pastoralist will try to abide by customs and rules that enable everyone to share the pasture. Such an arrangement may work reasonably satisfactorily for centuries because relative peace and communal redistribution arrangements keep the pastoralist society stable and prevent overgrazing. Then, however, comes the day of capitalist invasions, that is, the day when the undesired and culturally alien goal of accumulating wealth for its own sake is violently introduced and eventually becomes culturally accepted and pervasive. At this point, the inherent logic of capitalism remorselessly generates tragedy.

References:

Friedland, A., and R. Relyea. 2015. *Environmental Science for AP*. New York: W.H. Freeman & Co.

Hardin, G. 1968. The Tragedy of the Commons. *Science* 162 (3859): 1243-1248.

Hardin, G. 1974. Living on a Lifeboat. *Bioscience* 24 (10): 561-568.

Ostrom, E. 1990. *Governing the commons: the evolution of institutions for collective action*. Cambridge and New York: Cambridge University Press.

Ricoveri, G. 2013. *Nature for Sale: The Commons versus Commodities*. London: Pluto Press.

Roberts, R.S., and J. Emel. 1992. Uneven Development and the Tragedy of the Commons: Competing Images for Nature-Society Analysis. *Economic Geography* 68 (3): 249-271.

Sayre, N.F. 2008. The genesis, history, and limits of carrying capacity. *Annals of the Association of American Geographers* 98: 120–134.

Semchenko, M., M.J. Hutchings, and E.A. John. 2007. Challenging the tragedy of the commons in root competition: confounding effects of neighbour presence and substrate volume. *Journal of Ecology 95: 252-260.*

Wall, D. 2014. *The Commons in History. Culture, Conflict, and Ecology.* Boston: MIT Press.

Wenseleers, T., and F.L.W. Ratnieks. 2004. Tragedy of the Commons in *Melipona* Bees. *Proceedings: Biological Sciences* 271, Supplement 5: S310-S312.

Acknowledgements

Because so many have contributed so much to the development of ideas in this work, it would be impossible to recognize all the significant contributions. However, I would like to mention some of the most important ones.

First, I would like to thank Chris Kortright and Changing Sun Press for proposing the idea of publishing this book and for making it a reality. I am honored that it will be one of the first projects of that publishing project. I would also like to give special thanks to my many friends and fellow workers at the journal *Capitalism Nature Socialism*, in which the articles on which this work is based were first published. The idea of developing this extensive critique was suggested by Joel Kovel, Editor Emeritus of *CNS*, who also offered invaluable suggestions for its improvement. I am also very grateful to the current editor of *CNS*, Salvatore Engel-Di Mauro, for his encouragement and helpful suggestions, and for agreeing to write the introduction, despite his extremely heavy obligations. Beyond being ideal editors, Joel and Salvatore (Saed) have inspired me greatly by their exemplary theoretical and political work. Karen Charman of *CNS* did outstanding editorial work on the articles that improved this text greatly. I am grateful to all the members of the *CNS* Ecofeminist Collective, especially Ariel Salleh, and to other ecofeminist writers for *CNS*, including Sutapa Chattopadhyay, for their salutary influence on my thinking about global issues.

My conception of global issues was also greatly expanded and deeply transformed by a decade of involvement in the struggle of the people of West Papua against neo-colonialism, cultural genocide and ecological devastation. I am very grateful to have learned much about communal solidarity and the struggle for global justice from the Papuan people and from leaders such as Tom Beanal, head of LEMASA, the Amungme Tribal Council, Mama Yosepha Alomang, Papuan tribal leader and winner of Goldman Environmental Prize, and John Ondawame, international spokesperson for the Papuan people.

I am also deeply grateful for the many lessons I have learned about community, generosity, and compassion in action from the Tibetan Community in Dharamsala, India, with which I have been fortunate to spend considerable time over the last decade. Thanks to the Lha Charitable Trust, Ngawang Rabgyal, its director, Jampa Tsering, Tashi Dorjee, and, especially Ven. Tsering Phuntsok, our constant friend, guide and instructor for our month-long program in India. Thanks also to the Louisiana Himalaya Association, and Neil Guidry, its president, who have brought the Tibetan spirit of compassionate community to New Orleans, and introduced so many students and other volunteers to global service and solidarity.

My thanks also go to Francis Moore Lappé and the Food First Institute for being so instrumental in my early education about global food issues. I am also deeply grateful to ecofeminist theorists for developing a radical politics of care that has been of enormous importance to my studies and research. I am indebted in particular to the work of Vandana Shiva and Maria Mies, and once again to Ariel Salleh, especially for *Ecofeminism as Politics*, which was a major theoretical breakthrough almost two decades ago, and has been for me an enduring point of reference. Arundhati Roy has been one of my most important educators concerning social, political and cultural issues in India.

As mentioned in the text, the words of former Jamaican Prime Minister Michael Manley helped awaken me to the harsh realities of global economics and neo-colonialism at a key point in my own development. The works of Mike Davis, especially *Late Victorian Holocausts* and *Planet of Slums*, have been of major importance in my global ethics classes over the years, as is reflected in the discussion here. I have also been influenced strongly by the recent flowering of theoretical analysis and empirical study of the commons. Of greatest importance has been the groundbreaking research of Eleanor Ostrom, and Peter Linebaugh's magnificent work, *The Magna Carta Manifesto*.

I am grateful to Prof. Randall Amster of Georgetown University, Dr. Drew Chastain of Loyola University, Guy Henoument of the New Orleans Convivium, Prof. Leonard Kahn of Loyola University, Erin Lierl, poet, and Prof. Ian Smith of Washburn University for offering helpful comments. I also want to express my deep gratitude to my global ethics students at Loyola University New Orleans and in the Loyola Summer program in Dharamsala, India, for their thoughtful responses in their journal entries, and for many stimulating exchanges in class discussions over the years.

Finally, I want to thank the members of the grass-roots recovery communities with which I worked in the wake of Hurricane Katrina. They transformed my ideas of what things are of most urgent importance. They taught me so much about the deeper meaning of tragedy, hope, and solidarity.

The Tragedy of Common Sense

Part One: The Power of Myth

"It is necessary to follow the common; but although the Logos is common the many live as though they had a private understanding."
   –Heraclitus[1]

      The topic of this discussion will be both the common and the commons. It is about the truth we hold in common, and about certain falsehoods that we hold in common. These falsehoods, which inhabit both our minds and our way of being, are called "ideology." The particular object of ideology that will be investigated here is the commons. The commons consists of the places, and, indeed, the world that we hold in common, and which we have, in many ways, forsaken. This investigation aims at uncovering some of the ways in which ideology tears apart what is common and lays waste to the commons. Its subject is, in effect, the tragedy of ideology.

      One of the best known and most influential arguments in contemporary applied ethics is biologist Garrett Hardin's case for "lifeboat ethics," an analysis of the moral dimensions of world hunger, foreign aid, immigration policy, and population growth. Hardin describes "lifeboat ethics" as an application to these issues of his well-known concept of the "tragedy of the commons."[2] In a highly influential article with that title, Hardin used the term to depict a situation in which members of a group are able to exploit some common resource for their individual benefit, and in which the results are a degradation of the resource and serious harm for all members of the group.[3]

Hardin contends that such a situation is occurring globally in relation to food resources and population growth. He argues that the world is headed toward a catastrophic crisis in which global population will reach an unsustainable level that greatly exceeds "carrying capacity," and that many countries have already exceeded such capacity within their own borders. He asserts, further, that the primary cause of the impending global crisis is the rapid rate of population growth in poor countries, and that to avert disaster, it is essential that their fertility rates be reduced to the already modest and decreasing levels of many rich countries. In addition, he holds that food aid from rich to poor countries is a major factor in producing the unsustainably high fertility rates of the latter. More specifically, he argues that food aid causes a "ratchet effect" that prevents the population of a poor country from falling to a "carrying capacity" that would in his view "normally" constitute its limit, and instead allows it to overshoot this "carrying capacity" to an increasing degree that will ultimately occasion global collapse. His conclusion is that citizens of rich countries have no moral obligation to send food aid to poor countries, even in cases of severe famine. Indeed, the clear implication is that it is their moral duty *not* to do so.

A goal of the present discussion is to demonstrate the need for a dialectical social ecological analysis of the interconnections between phenomena such as world population growth, food resources, poverty and social inequality. This will be done through a critique of Hardin's non-dialectical, ahistorical, ideologically conditioned analysis and a consideration of why it has been so influential in the American academic subculture, in the larger American political culture, and particularly in some segments of the contemporary environmental movement. It is hoped that such a critique will contribute to understanding more clearly the processes through which ideology shapes political culture—and to finding ways to reverse such processes.

Part One of this discussion will include several steps. We will begin with some thoughts on the nature of ideology and the ways in which the reception of Hardin's ideas might tell us something about how ideology functions in contemporary society in general, and in academia in particular. Next, we will analyze in some detail both Hardin's lifeboat metaphor as a depiction of global society and his "ratchet effect" as an account of the impact of food aid on population. And lastly, we will look at Hardin's success as a prophet of demographic doom, and the ways in which his concept of carrying capacity relates to real-world social and demographic conditions.

We Hold These Falsehoods To Be Self-Evident

As a result of his iconoclastic and polemical articles, especially "The Tragedy of the Commons," Hardin became one of the most famous and most quoted American intellectuals. He won many awards for his work, including the Phi Beta Kappa award for science writing for the general public, in recognition of his outstanding communication skills. A Garrett Hardin Society was established in his honor.[4] "The Tragedy of the Commons" has been called "one of the most famous essays of all time," and has achieved wide recognition in various areas of American science and social science. A Google search shows literally thousands of references to the work as "a classic article," "a classic essay," "a classic piece," etc., and as many as 300,000 references to its title concept. It is often described as one of the most frequently reprinted articles, and it has no doubt appeared in many more than the 111 anthologies that have long been cited by his admirers. The Garrett Hardin Society claims, not without reason, that it is "widely accepted as a fundamental contribution to ecology, population theory, economics and political science."[5] While this article has been Hardin's most famous work, "Lifeboat Ethics" has also had a huge influence. In particular, it is one of the most widely-reprinted articles in the field of applied ethics. It is almost inevitably included in sections of moral problems anthologies on global justice issues, and many, if not most, introductory ethics students will encounter it. It has appeared in at least seventeen such anthologies,[6] in addition to being frequently included in collections in more specialized fields, such as environmental ethics and global ethics.

The article that is most often used to "balance" Hardin's "Lifeboat Ethics" article in ethics anthologies is Peter Singer's famous essay "Famine, Affluence, and Morality,"[7] which was written shortly before Hardin's article. Singer defends a "marginal utility" position in which the existence of severe food scarcities in poor countries implies an obligation on the part of affluent people to donate to food aid and famine relief up to the point that further giving would reduce donors to the level of suffering of famine victims. When presented with these two positions as the foremost "living options" in the ethics of world hunger, students are trapped in a moral dilemma that begs the question of the ability of poor countries to provide for their own food needs. The two sides of the dilemma are stark contrasts: either Singer's Draconian "marginal utility" option of reducing oneself to poverty by sending food to poor countries, or Hardin's "tough-love" option of doing nothing to help while allowing the hungry to suffer and die "for their own good." It is not difficult to imagine which choice will seem more plausible on the basis of such a superficially fair and balanced philosophical inquiry into a major contemporary moral issue.

A question that remains in the background of this discussion is that of the process by which certain texts emerge as canonical works in a field such as global ethics. Such a question deserves further investigation as part of a more general inquiry into the role of ideology in political culture. Why, one might ask, do certain articles appear habitually in ethics anthologies? Out of the hundreds of significant and illuminating articles relevant to the ethics of world population issues, why have Peter Singer's and Garrett Hardin's analyses emerged as two of the main options, and sometimes the only options, presented to students? Among the reasons are the following: 1) There is a preference for "point counterpoint" articles on ethical issues, so that an impression of fairness and objectivity, as defined by the dominant academic consensus, can be created; 2) For pedagogical reasons, there is a preference for articles with a simple argumentative structure that can be analyzed logically and tested for obvious fallacies; 3) Philosophy instructors' background and training are often rather narrowly analytical or formalist, with a bias toward conceptual analysis, as opposed to theoretical approaches that are historically and empirically grounded.[8] Many introductory-level ethics courses are assigned to graduate assistants and junior faculty who have increasingly been under pressure to pursue narrow and technical areas of specialization and publication, which is not conducive to broad general knowledge of issues in social ethics.[9]

As intriguing as these general questions concerning the place of ideology in academia may be, a more central concern here is the ways in which typical reactions to Hardin's acclaimed essays, and "Lifeboat Ethics" in particular, show the marks of ideology. When one is in the thralls of an ideological system, ideas that reflect strongly the core value commitments and reality conceptions of that ideology take on an aura of self-evidence. One immediately forgets the empirical evidence that contradicts those ideas, no matter how obvious and familiar that evidence may be. One overlooks the most blatant contractions between those ideas and one's other beliefs concerning value and reality. In short, a pervasive process of ideological blocking systematically distorts one's thinking and evaluating. As will be demonstrated, the ubiquity of the evidence against Hardin's thesis attests to the power of the dominant ideology, the dominant imaginary, the dominant system of habitual practices, and the dominant social structure. Scattered information about states of affairs has little force in the face of a dream world of powerful images and habitually reinforced ideas that form part of a comprehensive system of embodied reality. In this context, the ideological dream world[10] has the virtue of cohering with a larger world that appears powerfully real, while messages about some possibly existent alternate worlds (global society, the biosphere) can be largely filtered out as background noise.

What is it within the collective ideology and imaginary that resonates so well with the ideas and images presented by Hardin? The images in the media of thousands of helpless, often emaciated famine victims during occasional severe food crises have a great impact on the imagination.[11] On the other hand, the unimaginable reality of a billion victims of chronic malnutrition will have no place in the social imaginary. The public knows in some vague way that large amounts of money are disbursed for foreign aid, and in an ideological climate that interprets the allocation of social goods as a series of zero-sum games, most will only assume that significant amounts of this aid must be given to the undeserving poor of the world, and that such an appropriation of their taxes must be much to their own detriment.

The racist ideology and the racist imaginary that

objectify domestic minority groups as lazy, criminal, breeding animalistically, greedy for handouts, parasitical—and, of course, dirty—is enormously powerful. Such ideological and imaginary processes famously resulted in almost identical images of scavenging survivors of the Katrina disaster being labeled images of "looters" in the case of blacks and images of "finders" in the case of whites. The racist concepts and images of blacks and Latinos/Latinas, with all their accompanying baggage of fear and resentment, are easily transferred to and projected on the poor, largely non-white masses of the global South. We will consider how such transference is relevant to the generation of the ideological world of "lifeboat ethics."

The Power of Abstraction

For over 30 years my students have been reading Garrett Hardin's "Lifeboat Ethics" essay. I have always been struck by the powerful impact that Hardin's article, and his lifeboat metaphor in particular, have had on them. The majority of the students have been working adults from working-class and lower middle-class backgrounds, with a significant representation of ethnic minorities. However, there have also been many traditional-age students from more affluent backgrounds. Over the years, whatever the students' backgrounds and whatever their reservations about some of Hardin's views may have been, they have consistently judged his arguments to be strong and well-grounded in facts about the world. Why, we might ask, do Hardin's ideas exert such a powerful force, even among those who resist them? Why do his arguments tend to convince, even though they are quite weak? Why is his approach perceived as factually based, when almost all of his claims about states of affairs in the world are groundless, and can be seen to be groundless on the basis of even the most limited knowledge of conditions in the world? I would suggest that the answer is that they tap into aspects of the dominant ideology in a very powerful way and that they are therefore a good guide to understanding the nature of that ideology and its grip on the general consciousness.[12]

Some examples of comments by recent students illustrate the power of Hardin's depiction of human nature and the world. A considerable number of students accept his position with enthusiasm. One states that "Hardin's argument is valid" because "people who are always helped in times of need are going to become dependent on that cushion that is always provided for them." Another supports the idea of helping those in need, but fears that "if everyone gives too much, the lower classes will never get out of poverty and hunger, for they will get used to this system and never learn to maintain themselves or their families by their own." A third agrees with this, adding that "if everyone looks to others for help when times are tough, people will get lazy and turn to others for a bailout all the time," and that "if there is a shortcut or a way to get out of doing work, most people will take it." One student judges Hardin's ideas to be "much more practical" than those of other analysts of global problems, and adds that "his diagrams give good insight into why countries are the way they are and what needs to be done." The student notes that if Hardin's prescriptions are followed, "people will die, which many people with hearts will care about and fight to save, but the fact is that once these mass amounts of people die, a country will be down to a more manageable population." Another student agrees with Hardin that "if we stick to the Christian ideals and help everyone in need, then we will all perish in the end. We must make these countries stop reproducing at such a large rate so that they can sustain the population they already have."

What I find especially striking is that many students who have mixed feelings about Hardin's views, and even some who find them disturbing, feel compelled in the end to accept the validity of his position because of what they see as its factual, common-sense basis. One student comments that "the lack of recognition of the world's poor people is immoral," but "to give large amounts of food to poor people does result in increased population." This student, like a number of others, praises Hardin's "Ratchet Effect" theory (which will be discussed in detail later), saying that "it is logical" to conclude that "when the resources are there the population will grow no matter what the circumstances." In another case, a student finds Hardin's views "a little extreme," but notes that "he has good research behind his arguments." Another who has reservations concedes that Hardin "provides factual, useful information." One describes Hardin's analysis as "harsh wisdom," commenting that "unfortunately it is hard to dispute his logic, as much as I'd prefer to believe in the ideal outlook." This student explains that Hardin shows that "the first responsibility must go to the protection of your own lifeboat" and that "debilitating yourself for the sake of trying to help others makes the whole effort a vain attempt." Finally, a student states bluntly that Hardin's outlook is not "a very moral way to look at things," but concludes that nevertheless "he has a good point" in arguing that giving aid to "poor or vulnerable people or countries" means that "they will never be able to grow on their own."

The Scandal of Particularity

A crucial point in the development of my own awareness of global realities occurred when I was fortunate enough to hear a speech by Jamaican Prime Minister Michael Manley when he visited my university over thirty years ago. He was preceded by a representative of a group that was helping collect food for a ship coming down the Mississippi River picking up supplies to distribute to the poor in the Caribbean. Manley expressed his gratitude for such generosity, but made it clear that what Jamaica really needed was not canned goods, but rather assistance in making the transition to an economy that helped Jamaicans fulfill their own needs and develop their own possibilities. He observed that for a long time sugar cane production was central to the Jamaican economy; it was still a major sector when he spoke (the highest level of production was as late as 1965). However, given the declining value of sugar cane in the world economy, the more Jamaica continued to rely on this traditional crop the poorer it would become. What Jamaica needed was not charity, but rather the means to overcome such a legacy of the colonial past and the ability to shape its own future.

Manley's speech made an indelible impression on me, and I have often mentioned it to my ethics students. When discussing the Jamaican case study, I usually pose the question of why Jamaicans would have continued to remain heavily dependent on a product such as sugar cane when doing so was so detrimental to their position in the global economy. Usually the first, most spontaneous responses are that Jamaicans must have liked producing sugar cane, or that it's hard to break a habit. In other words, the answers follow the dominant ideology, in which it is the choice of the oppressed themselves that is at the root of their own oppression. Similar thinking often underlies the common observation that if people in poor countries did not *choose* to work in sweatshops they would not apply in large numbers for jobs in such workplaces, or continue to work there.

However, it does not take long for students to realize that working in cane fields would probably not be anyone's first choice of occupation, much less that of a large labor force. Some remember that it is the traditional form of forced labor at the notorious Louisiana State Penitentiary at Angola, and for many is a synonym for onerous labor. The next response, that sugar cane production is a habit (often "it's what they know how to do"), is, of course, correct. But students soon realize that the fact that something is a habit does not explain why it is this and not something else that has become habitual, or why although habits are often broken this one has continued for such a very long time. They see that the explanation is essentially circular, since it simply states that those who do it do it because it is what they do, without introducing any explanatory factors. The next suggestion is usually that the country's climate determines that this crop should predominate. Such reasoning does seem to have a certain empirical basis, since sugar cane does in fact grow well in tropical Jamaica, as it does in subtropical Louisiana. But almost everyone soon realizes that in Jamaica, as in Louisiana, many economic activities other than sugar production are possible, and while Louisiana has largely broken with such old habits as heavy dependence on sugar cane or cotton production, Jamaica has not. Thus, there must be some further explanation for such continued specialization in the case of Jamaica.

What is interesting from the standpoint of critique of ideology is that students' first responses typically attribute oppression to the free choice of the oppressed, and when this approach fails to hold up under examination, the next responses typically attribute it to something over which no one has control. The failure of these seemingly reasonable, natural, common-sense explanations points in the direction of another unreasonable and unnatural explanation that defies common sense. If the oppression is not chosen by the oppressed themselves, and it is not caused by conditions that exclude choice, it must be caused by the choice of someone other than the oppressed. The turning point occurs when it becomes apparent that a narrow focus on the present will not result in an *explanation*, as opposed to a *redescription*, of what

14

exists, and that consequently the details of history have to be examined. Many students have some familiarity with the Middle Passage and of the place of Jamaica in the economy of slave-trading, sugar cane planting, and rum production. Once these are mentioned, more recent social realities, including the neo-colonial economy built on the foundation of past slavery, quickly begin to make more logical and historical sense. The students begin to understand in concrete terms how the past can not only "weigh like a nightmare on the brains of the living,"[13] but indeed weigh like the iron shackles of slavery on their bodies.

The Ship of Foolishness

According to Hardin's lifeboat metaphor, "each rich nation amounts to a lifeboat full of comparatively rich people" while poor nations are "other, much more crowded, lifeboats" (71). Since their lifeboats cannot hold them, they "continuously fall out of their lifeboats and swim for a while in the water outside, hoping to be admitted to a rich lifeboat, or in some other way to benefit from the 'goodies' on board"[14] (71). Thus, according to Hardin's scenario, we are to imagine the rich on their lifeboats, merrily enjoying life, while the poor flounder miserably and helplessly at sea, struggling for survival. A rather curious aspect of this metaphor is that all this desperate floundering on the part of the poor does not prevent them from managing to reproduce at very high rates, as Hardin notes with alarm.

However, what is more crucial to the fate of the metaphor is other activities of these supposed flounderers that are ignored entirely by Hardin. This includes producing large quantities of agricultural products and, increasingly, manufactured goods that are exported to wealthy consumer societies such as Hardin's own. So were we to try to salvage this rapidly sinking metaphor we would need not only to imagine the poor of the world swimming around the ocean while reproducing prodigiously, but we would also have to imagine them at the same time throwing enormous quantities of goods on to the lifeboats. However, our job is not in fact to salvage it, but rather to investigate further whether it can remain afloat.

According to Hardin's account, the poor in the poorer countries of the world will have little chance of getting on local lifeboats, so they must attempt instead to somehow get aboard one of the richer ones. In more literal terms, this means that they would seek relatively lucrative jobs in the developed world. As we will see, Hardin's analysis of this problem depends heavily on his view that the problem of scarcity in poor countries stems from their tendency to continually exceed "carrying capacity," so that the poor must seek resources elsewhere, either by emigrating to rich countries or by demanding aid from these countries.

According to Hardin "each lifeboat is effectively limited in capacity," or, in more literal terms, "the land of every nation has a limited carrying capacity" (71). In view of his singling out of poor nations for exceeding "carrying capacity," it is somewhat surprising that he also concedes that this is a general global condition, for in so doing he veers dangerously in the direction of global realities. "We have already exceeded the carrying capacity of the land. We have been living on 'capital'—stored petroleum and coal—and soon we must live on income alone" (71). And this is indeed true of a global society based on fossil fuel consumption and the destruction and degradation of the planet's ecosystems. So at this point we discover that in Hardin's ideological dream world some societies are reproached for irresponsibly increasing their population and thus exceeding their "carrying capacity," while at the same time *all* societies are *already* exceeding their "carrying capacity."[15]

Hardin does not mention another (for him quite

embarrassing) implication if we follow this line of reasoning: industrialized societies that support their growth heavily through enormous per capita consumption of fossil fuels are then *exceeding carrying capacity much more* than poorer societies that consume little of such resources per capita.[16] Instead, he hopes that we will overlook this unfortunate implication and concentrate instead on the idea that it is poor societies that exceed "carrying capacity." To describe "our" position in the world ("we" being, of course, the citizens of affluent societies) he suggests that we imagine that we are on a lifeboat that holds 50 people, and has a maximum capacity of 60. However, he cautions, actually allowing the ten additional people onboard and reaching maximum capacity would violate the "engineering principle" of the "safety factor." Let it not be said that Hardin is not a man of principle.

Hardin presents scenarios for three possible responses to the lifeboat predicament as it relates to the question of immigration. The first scenario is based on what he calls "the Christian ideal of being 'our brother's keeper,'"[17] or the "Marxian ideal" of "from each according to his abilities, and to each according to his needs"[18] (72). Adopting such principles, he says, would mean inviting everyone onto the boat and thereby quickly sinking it, or, as he states it, "complete justice, complete catastrophe" (72). The implication is that no one foolishly tempted by Christian and Marxist principles could possibly hold on to them in the face of grim reality. A second possibility, for the more faint-hearted altruist, would be to allow others to board the boat until the maximum capacity is reached. However, in Hardin's view, this option only delays the process of collective suicide. With the "safety factor gone," before long a large wave will sink the boat and the result will be equally catastrophic (72). This leaves only a third choice, the one that cannot be refused if you live in lifeboat land. It is to allow no one to board the boat (with the possible exception of a few who bring along valuable wealth and talents) and to protect it against "boarding parties" (72).

Hardin thus presents the reader with a mytho-logical world in which human society consists of a war of all who are on lifeboats against all who are not, and in which lifeboat preservation is the first law of nature. He can then make the reasonable and non-controversial as-sumption that his generally affluent readers are averse to being drowned (thrown into poverty) and will therefore enthusiastically accept choice number three. It will be ob-vious that those on a lifeboat should defend themselves and what they possess against those outside the lifeboats, whether by denying entry to outsiders or by refusing to distribute to those outsiders any of the largesse, "the goodies," on the lifeboat (71). In more literal terms, this means that those who are not hopelessly in the grips of an irrational death wish founded on the most insidious altruism will oppose any programs to allow immigration or to send food aid to famine victims.[19]

Hardin relies largely on the myth of the lifeboat to guide his readers to these conclusions. His next step is to convince his audience of the absolute identity between myth and reality. He thus proposes to "enrich the im-age step by step with substantive additions from the real world" (73). As we will soon see, his major effort at "en-richment" consists of a cursory look at reproduction rates and some speculation about where trends seemed to him to be going at the time that he wrote. Fortunately, we now have almost four decades of actual history to examine in assessing Hardin's merits as a demographic prophet.

Hardin's Ratchet Job

First, however, it is important to analyze what is perhaps the most powerful aspect of Hardin's argu-ment after the lifeboat image itself. This is an ingenious pseudo-scientific analysis of an imaginary process called "the Ratchet Effect." The immediate context is an attack on a proposed "international food bank," but his target is any system of ongoing aid to famine victims. His thesis is that food aid interferes with a natural process in which population adjusts to the resources (essentially, merely the food supply) available within a country. He argues that in "a world inhabited by individually responsible sovereign nations, the population of each nation would repeatedly go through a cycle" (79) represented in the following chart:

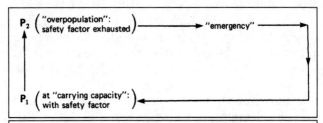

Figure 1. The population cycle of a nation that has no effective, conscious population control, and which receives no aid from the outside. P_2 is greater than P_1.

Hardin explains that this chart represents "the population cycle of a nation that has no effective, conscious population control, and which receives no aid from the outside" (80). The ideas presented are quite simple ones, so one might wonder why such a chart is necessary. It is a bit like creating a chart to explain a process such as "the normal human temperature cycle." At "T_1" X's temperature is "at normal level," but when it increases to "T_2," X's temperature is "high," after which X "takes aspirin," and if you follow the arrows carefully, you will discover that X's temperature returns to "normal level."

Of course, the chart is not necessary to illustrate such simple ideas; however, the use of a "figure" with seemingly technical variables such as "P_1" and "P_2" creates a useful aura of scientific authenticity and helps disguise the fact that in this case it is based on no empirical evidence at all. Interestingly, Hardin claims that "P_2 is greater than P_1, either in absolute numbers or because a deterioration of the food supply has removed the safety factor and produced a dangerously low ratio of resources to population" (79). Thus, P_2, a certain level of "overpopulation" beyond "carrying capacity" may actually represent a *decrease* in population resulting from a "deterioration of the food supply" because of "e.g., a crop failure" (79). Since this is only "e.g.," it may be because of *something else* that might produce such a result. We will consider later what this "something else" might be. At this point, we will merely observe that according to Hardin, overpopulation occurs when the population has either *increased* above "carrying capacity" or has not *decreased* quickly enough under the pressure of scarcity and is therefore still above "carrying capacity." Hardin observes that "if the 'emergency' is not met by outside help, the population drops back to the 'normal' level—the 'carrying capacity' of the environment—or even below" (79). This process is what is often described by partisans of such neo-Malthusianism as "letting nature take its course."

Hardin contends that if "poor countries that are governed by rulers insufficiently wise and powerful" are given food in times of "emergency," then "the population *cycle* of Figure 1 will be replaced by the population *escalator* of Figure 2. The input of food from a food bank acts as the pawl of a ratchet, preventing the population from retracing its steps to a lower level" (80-81). He argues that eventually poor countries will put so much pressure on the whole system that the final result will be "the total collapse of the whole system, producing a catastrophe of scarcely imaginable proportions" (81). [See Figure 2][20]

Hardin concludes that "under the guidance of this ratchet, wealth can be steadily moved in one direction only, from the slowly-breeding rich to the rapidly-breeding poor,

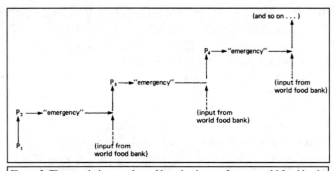

Figure 2. The population escalator. Note that in- put from a world food bank acts like the pawl of a ratchet, preserving the normal population cycle shown in Figure 1 from being completed. Pn+1 is greater than Pn, and the absolute magnitude of the "emergencies" escalates. Ultimately the entire system crashes. The crash is not shown, and few can imagine it.

the process finally coming to a halt only when all countries are equally and miserably poor" (81). The fact that wealth in the real world has typically moved "in one direction"— from poor to rich areas of the world—appears nowhere in Hardin's fantastic depiction of reality. Most incredibly, the ratchet theory assumes that those who have laid claim to and benefitted from disproportionate access to the resources of others will altruistically give away those resources out of feelings of unbounded generosity. According to Hardin's scenario, even as they see their food resources dwindling and begin spiraling toward disaster they will obsessively and self-destructively continue to support a huge dependent global population.[21] But in which world are such things conceivable? Here, as at many points, Hardin's position betrays its ideological nature most blatantly through the fact that it does not merely distort reality, but rather presents an absolute inversion of reality. Hardin offers his readers the ideological challenge. To paraphrase a classic formulation, if there be anything which to our eyes appears white and ideology defines it as black, we are to pronounce it black. And Hardin has found multitudes of readers with excellent ideological pronunciation.

Hardin's People Problem

Hardin's analysis of global population issues fails above all in the face of one embarrassing reality that steadfastly defies his ideological abstractions: the *people* who make up the *populations*. Just as real humans—being complex historical, spiritual and material beings—defy classical and neo-classical economics by failing to act as economistic abstractions, they defy Hardin's Neo-Malthusianism by failing to reproduce according to his ideological fantasies. He asserts confidently that "in the absence of population control by a sovereign, sooner or later the population grows to P_2 ['over-populated']" (79).

Yet, he could easily have found masses of counterevidence had he ventured into the realm of modern and contemporary history. The enormous demographic changes that had already taken place in much of Europe and other parts of the world when he wrote this statement had not been caused by "population control by a sovereign," or, as he states it elsewhere, by a system of "conscious population control" (80). In fact, a country such as France, which without such "conscious population control" saw its fertility rate drop below replacement level, had already "consciously" adopted pronatalist policies aimed at encouraging families to have a third child.[22] Long-term tendencies that began in Europe were, even as he wrote, beginning to spread much more widely across the globe.

It is instructive to look closely at Hardin's predictions of demographic doom alongside what has actually happened in the world over the three-and-a-half decades during which his essay was busy becoming a classic. He notes that the populations of wealthy nations were doubling every 87 years while those of other poor nations were doing so every 35 years. He then proposes a little thought experiment. He states that the United States had, at the time that he wrote, 210 million people, which, he notes, was equal to the combined populations of Colombia, Venezuela, Ecuador, Morocco, Thailand, Pakistan, and the Philippines. However, the US population was increasing by only .8 percent per year, while the population of the other eight countries was increasing by 3.3 percent each year (73).

He then has the reader imagine that by the time that the U.S. population will have doubled to 420 million, his other carefully-selected countries will then have a combined population of 3.54 billion. He confronts the reader with the presumably disturbing prospect that there will be eight people from those countries enviously eyeing the American lifeboat for every American on it. He open-mindedly concedes to the naïve that trends can change for the better, perhaps in some airy world of logical possibility. But he concludes tough-mindedly that in the real world it seems much more likely that rates of increase will fall faster in rich countries. So the danger is that the actual future will probably be "even worse" than the projection, and in view of this, any ethic of "sharing" will be "even more suicidal" (74). We will never be allowed to forget the genocidal implications of any altruistic inclinations we may be clinging to, if Hardin can do anything about it.

Since it has now been over 40 years since Hardin made his predictions, we might, then, look at what has happened in the countries that he chose to help make his case. Recent (2014) rates of annual population increase in these countries are: Colombia, 1.07 percent; Venezuela, 1.42 percent; Ecuador, 1.37 percent; Morocco, 1.02 percent; Thailand, 0.35 percent; Pakistan 1.49 percent; and the Philippines, 1.81[23] percent. The growth rate for the United States, after rather ironically bucking the trend and increasing, is now at .77 percent, only slightly below the rate that Hardin cited. Even as the U.S. rate has remained relatively stable, the rates of the other countries, which Hardin predicted would "fall more slowly" than that of the U.S., have dropped quite radically, from an average of about 3.3 percent to an average of about 1.2 percent. And while Hardin could blithely assume that in the absence of significant food aid there would be relatively consistent rates of increase for such countries for a period of 87 years, this precipitous drop has taken place in less than half that span of time. It should be noted that these countries are not the sites of the most severe food crises over this period. In fact, many countries which have seen extreme scarcity during the intervening period have, in fact, much higher rates of increase. A recent report for the FAO cited four countries in which there is an "exceptional shortfall in aggregate food production/supplies."[24] These are the Central African Republic, Gambia, Guinea-Bissau, and Senegal. These countries have fertility rates of 4.46, 3.85, 4.30, and 4.51, respectively.[25] These countries also have high growth rates relative to other countries, 2.13, 2.23, 1.91, and 2.48, respectively. Thus, if one examines food resource and fertility statistics over time, it is clear that food scarcity and death from malnutrition correlate with continued high fertility rates and growth rates relative to other countries, which is just the opposite of what Hardin's analysis predicts.

While Hardin foresaw a world in which for a long period of time only the threat of famine would deter most nations from sustaining growth rates on the order of 3.3 percent, the global growth rate after 42 years was about 1.14 percent, not drastically greater than the .8 percent in the US. By 2014 the global fertility rate had fallen to 2.33, only slightly higher than that of the United States, and India's had fallen to 2.51.[26] Garrett Hardin's own fertility rate was, by the way, 4.0.

For Hardin, such global developments were simply unthinkable. In "Lifeboat Ethics" he rejects with disdain the idea that aid to poor countries might help them go through the "benign demographic transition" that has been seen throughout the developed world. He says that "those who believe in the benign demographic transition dismiss the pejoristic mechanism of Figure 2 in the belief that each input of food from the world outside fosters development within a poor country thus resulting in a drop in the rate of population increase" (82). However, such a belief, which would be as simplistic as Hardin's own view, is certainly not the position of advocates of developmental justice. Their position is, first, that food scarcity does not, in fact, correlate with declines in fertility (except temporarily in cases of severe famine) and, secondly, that food aid can often be part of a many-faceted program of just, sustainable, and participatory development that does correlate with declines in fertility rates.

Hardin claims that "there are many counter examples" to the theory of benign demographic transition (82). But his examples are based largely on the temporary phenomenon of the post-WWII baby boom and do not reflect larger trends. Later developments have gone in a direction precisely opposite the one he predicted. One-third of the countries in the world now have fertility rates below the replacement rate of 2.1 and two-thirds now have fertility rates below 3. India's fertility rate is now 2.81, which is lower than the US fertility rate was as recently as 1945-1964, shortly before Hardin's "lifeboat" article was written. The post-WWII high in the United States, when Garrett Hardin was beginning his academic career, was 3.8. He noted with alarm in his article that "the average population growth is over 2 percent and shows no signs of slackening" (82). Yet, it had, in fact, been "slackening" for three years, and had slipped below 2 percent the very year that his article was published. Since then it has decreased significantly to only 1.13 percent by 2009.[27] To summarize the evidence, many countries that have never been subjected to the food scarcities that Hardin advocates have seen radical decreases in fertility rates. On the other hand, many countries that have seen such scarcities have maintained high fertility rates. Hardin's causal claims regarding food resources and fertility rates are thoroughly discredited and the correlation between these two variables turns out to be generally the reverse of the one that he claims to exist.

The Myth of Carrying Capacity

One of the most crucial ideological concepts in Hardin's analysis is "carrying capacity." Of course, "carrying capacity" is not a *mere* myth. In its original, biological sense it can function as a useful technical concept. According to a typical formulation, it is defined as "the equilibrium size at which a particular population in a particular environment will stabilize when its supply of resources (including nutrients, energy, and living space) remains constant."[28] But when the concept is used to link the occurrence of famine to a supposed surplus of human beings within the borders of a given nation-state, one leaves the realm of biology and enters that of ideology and political mythology. It crosses the same line that was crossed when Darwinian science was transformed into Social Darwinist ideology, for similar reasons and with similar results. It follows the iron law of ideology as it operates within the society of domination. It is the survival of what fits.

One necessarily begins to suspect Hardin's concept when one starts to test it in relation to the major phenomena of the past century to which it purports to be most relevant. What does one find if one inquires into the causes of famine in the 20th century in India, China, the Ukraine, Bangladesh, Biafra, Somalia, Ethiopia, Mozambique, East Timor and other prominent cases? It becomes clear that the most important factors have consistently been political and economic, and not demographic ones. In the majority of cases just listed, famine was the result of deliberate state policy, with goals such as enforcing the authority of the ruling regime, protecting economic interests, and most commonly, crushing dissident factions and separatist movements. In these cases, one finds that as soon as the political crisis was over, the food crisis also ended, "carrying capacity" miraculously expanded, and population began to increase.

Not only does Hardin fail to investigate the actual causes of famine, he also naïvely assumes that availability of food is the single variable relevant to declines in death rates. However, as Murdock and Oaten point out, in the real, empirical world such declines in mortality rate have in fact correlated strongly with factors such as "improved sanitation and medical advances," and therefore "cutting out food aid will not necessarily lead to population declines."[29] In addition, as has been mentioned, we know that absence of food aid does not correlate with declines in population growth, since many areas in which the populations do not receive it have the highest fertility rates and rates of population growth. Thus, cutting off food aid might give Hardin's neo-Malthusian followers a feeling of gratification at seeing what they perceive as the deserved suffering of the poor, inferior, and irresponsible segments of humanity, but it would not achieve the goals that they use to justify it. For Hardin's contrived "Ratchet Effect" to work they would have to find ways to reverse basic health and sanitation advances, not to mention other social achievements that help reduce mortality. Only then would we be able to return to Hardin's good old days of the "normal population cycle," in which large numbers of people died needlessly from poor sanitation, poor or non-existent health care, and poor diet.

Furthermore, if Hardin's thesis concerning population growth were correct, one might expect famine and malnutrition to correlate in some significant way with population density. When he refers to poor countries that he thinks to be "above carrying capacity" as "crowded nations," this would seem to imply that they are densely populated, while when he describes affluent countries as safely below "carrying capacity," one would think that they would be more sparsely populated. Yet some of the richest countries in the world—the ones that in Hardin's metaphor have large, uncrowded lifeboats—are in reality among the most densely populated. Using 2009 IMF rankings of 180 countries, the second most densely populated country, Singapore, is the 23rd richest, the third most densely populated, Malta, is the 35th richest, the fifth most densely populated, Bahrain, is the 31st richest, the 11th most densely populated, South Korea, is the 38th richest, and the 14th most densely populated, Holland, is the seventh richest. Other small states, such as Monaco, the most densely populated country, and Vatican City, the seventh most densely populated, are centers of great wealth. On the other hand, many countries that have seen the most severe malnutrition and famine (Hardin's "emergencies") are among the less densely populated ones: Ethiopia is 102nd; Eritrea, 134th; Mozambique, 148th; Sudan, 159th; Somalia, 169th; Congo, 176th; and Chad, 179th (to mention only a few of many examples).

Of course, these statistics are rather abstract. The complex reality is more striking. We find many examples of densely-populated countries that are incapable of fulfilling their own food needs, and are heavily dependent on imports for their food supply. In many cases, these are rich countries that have a high level of nutrition, and from Hardin's perspective have populations that are far below "carrying capacity." On the other hand, there are many countries that are sparsely populated, produce large quantities of agricultural products, and are heavy exporters of these products. In many cases, these are poor countries that suffer from widespread malnutrition, and from Hardin's perspective they have populations that are beyond "carrying capacity." Thus, Hardin's idea of "carrying capacity" is disconnected from what might seem most obviously relevant, the *realized* capacity to produce food that can support the lives of human beings.

It is also useful to reflect on the concept of "carrying capacity" as "capacity"—that is, as *potential* to support human lives. Coffin notes that we have the capacity to feed twice the world's population with present food resources, but that half of the world's grain is fed to cattle. He observes that according to some estimates, it takes sixteen pounds of grain to produce one pound of meat, so that meat production entails a policy of reducing effective food-production capacity for human beings. In addition, he says, energy resources are squandered in such production, since it takes 78 calories of fossil fuel to produce one calorie of beef protein, as opposed to only two calories of fossil fuel to produce one calorie of soy protein.[30]

This has obvious implications for vague Hardinesque speculation about "carrying capacity." If a country devotes a significant amount of land to raising cattle for export rather than to raising crops that are used for local subsistence, the domestic hunger and malnutrition that result from such an allocation has nothing to do with exceeding any hypothetical "carrying capacity," and much to do with a failure to realize a real capacity to fulfill the needs of the local people. And this is what so often happens when production is organized under conditions of concentrated economic and political power and monopolistic control of land. Actually realized capacity (to produce necessities of life) is turned into an incapacity (to fulfill "effective" needs) that is engineered for the sake of profit and power. The manner in which "lifeboat ethics" follows the classic model of ideological processes is almost breathtaking. In "The Power of Money in Bourgeois Society" the young

Marx famously observed: "Does not my money transform all my incapacities into their contrary?"[31] Perhaps never has there been a more striking example than "lifeboat ethics" of the manner in which capital, through the magic of ideology, turns the productive capacities of humanity and nature into their very contrary.

There is always a "Purloined Letter" quality to the secrets of ideology, and this is taken to the extreme in the present case. The global crime scene is veritably littered with incriminating evidence of the gap between a nation's actual food resources and the access of the populace to those resources. For example, the following appeared recently: "Just a few months ago, a drought-induced famine steadily spread toward Kenya from neighboring Ethiopia and Sudan threatening millions of lives in a lush, bountiful country that should be able to feed itself and more; at the same time, several top Kenyan politicians were implicated in a scheme to illegally sell off millions of pounds of the country's emergency grain reserves, at obscene profits."[32] While reports of such flagrant abuses appear periodically, they merely punctuate the larger ongoing story. The everyday, ordinary, quite legal diversion of essential food resources in poor countries for export to rich ones, for the benefit of a small privileged segment of the population, is a common and seemingly conspicuous phenomenon. Yet it is so ideologically conditioned that it seldom arouses conscious notice, much less any sense of indignation. Within the context of the practical, institutional, ideological and imaginary world order, it fades into the background and is ripe for mystification as "exceeding carrying capacity." Garrett Hardin was good enough to state his fundamental religious belief in the form of a commandment: "Thou shalt not transgress the carrying capacity."[33] However, the critique of ideology is concerned precisely with transgressing the boundaries established by such mythology. When one is able to break through the barriers set up by ideology, and formerly invisible conditions are brought into focus, the illusory nature of Hardin's sacrosanct concept becomes quite evident.

It should be noted that since Hardin's essay appeared, more coherent and rational concepts related to the general issue of "carrying capacity" have been developed. One such concept is that of the "global footprint," which is based on per capita use of ecological resources within any given geographical area, and is expressed in "global acres" of biological productive capacity used per capita.[34] Though this concept has been criticized for underestimating long-term ecological impact and the importance of relative wilderness areas, it gives a rough idea of relative use of resources in each country. According to the Global Footprint Network, the average person in the world is now using 1.9 global acres more than is available. In other words, there is a condition of "overshoot" in which ecological resources are being depleted globally by current overuse. However, the footprint varies greatly from country to country. Eleven countries have a deficit of over 10 global acres per capita. These are Israel, Kuwait, Qatar, Singapore, the UAE, Belgium, Greece, Spain, Switzerland, the UK, and the USA. Clearly, it is the affluent "lifeboat" countries that are the greatest drain on the planet's ecological resources and it is they that are making the greatest contribution to exceeding "carrying capacity" in any meaningful sense. Once again, we find that not only is reality distorted through the lens of ideology, it is transformed into its very opposite.

Notes

1. Heraclitus, Fragment 2 (Bywater number 92) in G.S. Kirk and J.E. Raven, *The Presocratic Philosophers* (Cambridge: Cambridge University Press, 1969), p. 188.

2. Garrett Hardin, "Living on a Lifeboat" in *BioScience*, Vol. 24, No. 10, 1974, pp. 561-568; online at the Garrett Hardin Society website at: http://www.garretthardinsociety.org/articles/art_living_on_a_lifeboat.html. All quotations from Hardin's argument come from this article, which is found in the appendix below. Page numbers in parentheses refer to the text in this volume.

3. Garrett Hardin, "The Tragedy of the Commons" in *Science*, Vol. 162, No. 3859, December 13, 1968, pp. 1243-1248. It has often been pointed out that reproductive decisions do not in fact follow this paradigm and that the situation that Hardin describes does not correspond to the historic institution of a "commons." Thus, his "application" of this concept to population issues is at best a vague and impressionistic one.

4. See the Garrett Hardin Society website at http://www.garretthardinsociety.org/ for links to many of Hardin's articles, biographical information, tributes to Hardin, and much additional material.

5. "Garrett James Hardin Curriculum Vitae" on Garrett Hardin Society website at http://www.garretthardinsociety.org/gh/gh_cv.html.

6. See for example: Raziel Abelson and Marie Louise Friquegnon, *Ethics for Modern Life*, 6th ed. (New York: Bedford/St. Martin's, 2002); Daniel Bonevac, *Today's Moral Issues*, 3rd ed. (New York: McGraw-Hill, 1998); Jeffrey R. Di Leo, *Morality Matters: Race, Class, and Gender in Applied Ethics* (New York: McGraw-Hill, 2002); Anthony Failkowski, *Moral Philosophy for Modern Life* (New York: Prentice Hall, 1997); Lawrence M. Hinman, *Contemporary Moral Issues: Diversity and Consensus*, 2nd ed. (New York: Prentice Hall, 1999); Christine M. Koggel, *Moral Issues in Global Perspective* (Peterborough, ON: Broadview Press, 1999); Thomas Mappes and Jane Zembaty, *Social Ethics: Morality and Social Policy* (New York: McGraw-Hill, 2006); Larry May, Shari Collins-Chobanian, and Kai Wong, *Applied Ethics: A Multicultural Approach* (New York: Prentice Hall, 2005); Jeffrey Olen, Julie C. Van Camp, and Vincent Barry, *Applying Ethics: A Text with Readings*, 8th ed. (Belmont, CA: Wadsworth Publishing, 2004); Louis P. Pojman, *Life and Death: A Reader in Moral Problems*, 2nd ed. (Belmont, CA: Wadsworth Publishing, 1999); Terrence Reynolds, *Ethical Issues: Western Philosophical and Religious Perspectives* (Belmont,

CA: Wadsworth Publishing, 2005); Stephen Satris, *Taking Sides: Clashing Views on Moral Issues*, 11th ed. (New York: McGraw-Hill/Dushkin, 2007); Christina Hoff Sommers and Fred Sommers, *Vice and Virtue in Everyday Life: Introductory Readings in Ethics* (Belmont, CA: Wadsworth Publishing, 2003); James P. Sterba, *Morality in Practice*, 5th ed. (Belmont, CA: Wadsworth Publishing, 1996); Mark Timmons, *Disputed Moral Issues: A Reader* (New York: Oxford University Press, 2006); Louis Vaughn, *Doing Ethics: Moral Reasoning and Contemporary Issues* (New York: W.W. Norton and Co., 2007); and James E. White, *Contemporary Moral Problems* (Belmont, CA: Wadsworth Publishing, 2005).

7. Peter Singer, "Famine, Affluence, and Morality" in *Philosophy and Public Affairs*, Vol. 1, No. 1, Spring 1972, pp. 229-243.

8. This distinction should not be identified with the conventional juxtaposition of "analytical" versus "Continental" (i.e., European subcontinental) philosophy. There are, of course, "analytical" philosophers who are engaged in empirical investigation and "Continental" philosophers who are narrowly formalistic. The issue is the degree to which a dialectical confrontation between theory and historical phenomena is undertaken.

9. This impression comes in part from reading hundreds of resumés of job applicants in recent years.

10. As used here, "ideological dream world" is shorthand for the more-than-ideological world determined not only by the dominant ideology, but by the dominant imaginary, the dominant ethos, and the dominant institutional structure. The subject constitutes a world (and is constituted by it) by thinking it, imagining it, living it, and beholding it.

11. Ionesco had great insight into the difference between acutely experienced personal trauma and the normal civilized response to distant tragedy: "If only it had happened somewhere else, in some other country, and we'd just read about it in the papers, one could discuss it quietly, examine the question from all points of view and come to an objective conclusion .... But when you're involved yourself, when you suddenly find yourself up against the brutal facts, you can't help feeling directly concerned—the shock is too violent for you to stay cool and detached. I'm frankly surprised, I'm very, very surprised. I can't get over it." *Rhinoceros and Other*

Plays (New York: Grove Press, 1960), pp. 78-79. The moral: If it happens somewhere else, we get over it.

12. The scope of this "consciousness" should be taken to include not only abstract ideas, but also emotions, feelings, mental dispositions, and "habits of mind" in a large sense.

13. As Marx phrases it in his famous words at the beginning of *The Eighteenth Brumaire of Louis Bonaparte* (Moscow: Progress Publishers, 1937); online at https://www.marxists.org/archive/marx/works/download/pdf/18th-Brumaire.pdf.

14. In reality, the vast majority of the poor of the world would not have fallen off, but would never have been on the lifeboats at all. Moreover, the elites of these poor nations probably do not feel very crowded on their lifeboats—consisting of their estates, rich neighborhoods, resorts, gated communities, and exclusive high-end malls.

15. It has become a commonplace in studies of planetary ecology that humanity has collectively "exceeded its carrying capacity," and is depleting rather than regenerating the earth's biotic wealth. For example, Wackernagel, et al., in a well-known analysis, claim that "whereas humanity's load [demand for 'natural capital'] corresponded to 70% of the biosphere's capacity in 1961, this percentage grew to 120% by 1999. In other words, a 20% overshoot means that it would require 1.2 earths, or one earth for 1.2 years, to regenerate what humanity used in 1999." See Mathis Wackernagel et al., "Tracking the ecological overshoot of the human economy" in *Proceedings of the National Academy of Sciences of the United States of America [PNAS]*, vol. 99 no. 14, pp. 9266–9271. It does not follow from this collective "overshoot," and neither is it true, that every country in the world is consuming at a level that would result in "overshoot" if its individual level of consumption were universalized. (See the discussion of "ecological footprint" below.) Neither does it follow from this collective "overshoot" that any given country is in a condition of "overshoot" in relation to the biotic productivity within its own borders.

16. As Robert Van Wyk asks rather pertinently, "Why should the Asian or African people be compared to the 'sheep' who are the greatest threat to the commons when the average American uses up thirty times the amount of the earth's resources as does the average Asian or African, and when the developed nations import

more protein from the developing nations than they export to them?" See "Perspectives on World Hunger and the Extent of our Positive Duties," in *Public Affairs Quarterly*, 2, 1988, p. 76.

17. Hardin is in general quite suspicious of the Christian tradition, but he makes an exception for the third-century theologian Tertullian, who is quoted as saying that "the scourges of pestilence, famine, wars, and earthquakes have come to be regarded as a blessing to overcrowded nations, since they serve to prune away the luxuriant growth of the human race" (79). The implication seems to be that humanity was already having problems with "carrying capacity" in certain nations over 1800 years ago, but Hardin fails to pursue this intriguing hypothesis, which might have suggested how little this elusive concept has to do with absolute numbers of human beings in relation to what is provided by the earth. On the other hand, what does emerge clearly from Hardin's theological digression is that beneath his contemptuous rejection of altruistic religious feelings lies a faith in a kind of bloodthirsty Providence that rules the world barbarically.

18. This saying, made famous by Marx's version of it in the "Critique of the Gotha Program," was already common to a century-long tradition of French utopians and socialists, and had been used most notably by Saint-Simon and Louis Blanc.

19. The present analysis will focus on the question of food aid to show that Hardin's presuppositions about conditions in the world are false and that his arguments are unsound, but a similar case can be made to show that his claims concerning immigration do not support his conclusions.

20. The process thus culminates in the neo-Malthusian fantasy of the sublimely cataclysmic demographic collapse.

21. One must wonder if Hardin might not have come under the spell of Ayn Rand, who was capable of imagining in *The Fountainhead* that "the world is perishing in an orgy of self-sacrifice."

22. See, for example, Marie-Thérèse Letablier, "Fertility and Family Policies in France," in *Journal of Population and Social Security*, "Supplement to Volume one," online at www.ipss.go.jp/webj-ad/Webjournal.files/population/2003_6/9.Letablier.pdf.

23. CIA World Factbook growth rate figures for 2014; online at https://www.cia.gov/Library/publications/the-world-factbook/fields/2002.html.

24. Food and Agriculture Organization of the United Nations (FAO), "Countries Requiring External assistance for Food" (March, 2105); online at http://www.fao.org/Giews/English/hotspots/index.htm.

25. CIA World Factbook fertility figures for 2014; online at https://www.cia.gov/library/publications/the-world-factbook/rankorder/rawdata_2127.txt.

26. CIA World Factbook fertility figures for 2014. It should be noted that Hardin was not a very good prophet in the area of global food production either. He judges that "whether or not the Green Revolution can increase food production is doubtful (Harris 1972, Paddock 1970, Wilkes 1972), but in any event not particularly important" (83). However, even severe critics of the Green Revolution agree that in many countries, especially in much of Asia and parts of Latin America, it helped food production increase much more rapidly than population did. Nevertheless, the benefits of this production often did not accrue to local populations, since the increase was in export crops that displaced subsistence ones, so that policies helped larger landowners and agribusiness while driving small farmers out of business. For a concise summary of some of these tendencies, see *World Hunger: Twelve Myths*, Ch. 5.

27. CIA World Factbook growth rate figures for 2009.

28. C. Starr and R. Taggart, *Biology: The Unity and Diversity of Life*, 5th ed. (Belmont, CVA: Wadsworth Publishing Co., 1981), "Glossary."

29. Murdoch and Oaten, p. 562.

30. Tristram Coffin, "World Food Supply: The Damage Done by Cattle-Raising" in *The Washington Spectator*, vol. 19, no. 2 (Jan. 15, 1993).

31. Karl Marx, *Economic and Philosophical Manuscripts of 1844* (Moscow: Progress Publishers, 1974), p. 121.

32. Jeffrey Gettleman, "East Africa: The Most Corrupt Country" in *New York Review of Books* Vol. LVII, No. 1 (Jan. 14, 2010), p. 35.

33. Garrett Hardin Society, "Garrett Hardin Quotations"; online at http://www.garretthardinsociety.org/info/quotes.html.

34. "The Ecological Footprint uses yields of primary products (from cropland, forest, grazing land and fisheries) to calculate the area necessary to support a given activity. Biocapacity is measured by calculating the amount of biologically productive land and sea area available to provide the resources a population consumes and to absorb its wastes, given current technology and management practices .... A nation's consumption is calculated by adding imports to and subtracting exports from its national production. Results from this analysis shed light on a country's ecological impact .... A country has an ecological reserve if its Footprint is smaller than its biocapacity; otherwise it is operating with an ecological deficit." See *Global Footprint Network Website*; online at http://www.footprintnetwork.org/. In February, 2016 the Global Footprint Network updated its calculations, finding that the global carbon footprint is 16% higher than previously thought, and that the overall global ecological footprint is 8% higher. The new national footprint data can be downloaded at http://www.footprintnetwork.org/en/index.php/GFN/page/public_data_package.

Part Two: From Ideology to Historical Reality

On Not Giving A Man A Fish

Much of Hardin's analysis of "lifeboat ethics" consists of a polemic against the evils of aid. And one must agree that there are, in fact, evils of aid. In his attack on food aid, Hardin claims that special interests have profited from aid, that aid sometimes pushes up food prices, and that aid programs create bureaucracies that tend to develop an interest in their own perpetuation. All of these contentions are correct. In fact, he could have added that food aid is often detrimental to domestic agriculture in recipient countries and makes their achievement of long-term food security more difficult. It is because of these and other serious problems (such as the fact that aid does not usually go to countries that need it most, and that when it does go to these countries, it does not go to the people who need it most) that the Food First Institute has suggested that countries that have received food aid would perhaps have been better off without it. These are not, however, as Hardin concludes, arguments against aid, since the option of distributing it wisely and justly has always existed, but rather an argument against the ineffectual or even destructive forms that aid has conventionally taken.

Unfortunately, Hardin's polemic misleads and

reinforces widespread misconceptions much more often than it reveals anything about the nature of aid. For example, it promotes the conventional but entirely erroneous view that the U.S. government distributes large amounts of food aid to the poor of the world. Hardin perpetuates the ideological cliché that foreign aid consists of uselessly throwing money at intractable problems, while at the same time unjustly taking away the hard-earned wealth of productive citizens. He notes that "in the years 1960 to 1970 a total of $7.9 billion was spent on the 'Food for Peace' program, and that during the years 1948 to 1970 an additional $49.9 billion were extracted from American taxpayers to pay for other economic aid programs, some of which went for food and food-producing machinery" (76). He complains that "though all U.S. taxpayers lost" by paying for such programs, "special interest groups gained handsomely" (76). He lists numerous groups that profited, ranging from farmers, to manufacturers, to the transportation industry. However, he is at a loss to imagine any rational justification that could have made such profiteering possible, blaming it instead on an obviously misguided and self-defeating humanitarianism. Thus, aid programs succeed in exploiting completely irrational emotions in order to make possible massive fraud and opportunism. In the end, "foreign aid has become a habit that can apparently survive in the absence of any known justification" (77).

In fact, some justifications are quite widely known. Amazingly, Hardin does not seem to have the slightest awareness of the rationale that has, in fact, been most commonly used to defend such programs—their role in the pursuit of global political and military policy and, essentially, the vaunted "national interest." He seems entirely oblivious to these programs' crucial role in exerting political influence around the world, and to the fact that they are often quite explicitly described as

39

instruments of foreign policy. He might have taken as a hint the fact that that so-called "developmental aid" and "humanitarian aid" have always had such a minimal correlation with real global food needs. He might have noticed that in the years preceding the publication of his article the poor country that was at the top of the list of foreign aid recipients was U.S.-occupied Vietnam, and that Israel, a very rich county, was already receiving more aid than any of the poor countries of the world other than Vietnam.[1] By the late 1970's, Israel and Egypt would be receiving about one-third of all foreign aid, and by the late 1980's they would be receiving about one-third of all economic or developmental aid. Poor countries with large populations and widespread malnutrition would be a competing for a small fraction of one percent of the total, while a single rich country with .01 percent of the world's population (Israel) would receive as much as most of them combined.[2]

Hardin reinforces the constantly repeated cliché that the United States is "the most generous country in the world." It is widely believed by Americans that the U.S. gives the most governmental and individual aid to the needy of the world, and such supposed over-generosity to wasteful and ungrateful foreigners is one of the stock right-wing arguments for slashing aid. A poll taken by the University of Maryland Program on International Policy Attitudes in the mid-90's showed that 75 percent of the U.S. public thought that foreign aid expenditures were excessive and that 64 percent wanted them cut. Respondents were asked how much of the federal budget they thought went to foreign aid, whether it should be either cut or increased, and, if so, how much. On average, they thought that foreign aid ate up 18 percent of the federal budget, and most responded that although it should be decreased drastically from its present level, reducing it to as little as 3 percent would be too great a cut. In fact, less than 1 percent of the budget was allocated to foreign aid at the time of the poll.³ Thus, the public thought that foreign aid should be slashed to an amount that was more than three times greater than its existing level. Despite this irony, the real message of the poll was that the illusion of vast generosity and enormous waste had been bought by the public.

The belief in American hyper-generosity, while ordinarily taken as a self-evident article of faith, is sometimes supported by reference to figures for U.S. gross giving, rather than those for per capita giving or giving as a percentage of Gross National Income. Such figures present overwhelming evidence that more aid emanates from the Unites States than from Luxembourg, for example. However, since the other affluent countries of the world have only a fraction of the U.S. population, gross figures are meaningless as a standard for generosity, even under the implausible assumption that the motive for most U.S. developmental aid is, in fact, generosity. Nevertheless, if we set aside considerations of altruism and take "generous" to mean simply "sending a lot," Americans are among the least generous, and are indeed perhaps the stingiest, of the citizens of affluent countries.

U.S. proportional contributions are dwarfed by those of many other countries. In one study of developmental aid, Norway was the biggest donor, giving .93 percent of its GNI. Among 22 developed nations, the United States was twenty-first in such aid, its .22 percent of GNI only slightly ahead of Portugal's .21 percent. Two countries gave more than four times as much per capita than the U.S., five gave more than three times as much, eleven gave more than twice as much, and 20 of the other 21 gave more per capita.⁴ A report on quality-adjusted aid, with aid expressed as percentage of Gross Domestic Product, showed the top twenty donors ranging from Sweden's .50 percent of GDP to the U.S.'s .07 percent. By this measure, one country gave over seven times as much as the U.S., three gave more than six times as much, four gave more than five times as much, seven gave more than triple, twelve gave more than double, and nineteen gave more than the U.S.[5]

For Hardin, such statistics would show only that other rich countries are even more addicted than is the U.S. to the evils of charity. And he is quite concerned that we understand just how evil charity is. He comments that "the demoralizing effect of charity on the recipient has long been known," after which he quotes that gem of conventional wisdom. "Give a man a fish and he will eat for a day; teach him how to fish and he will eat for the rest of his days" (83). This is the principle concerning helping those in need that has been most consistently quoted by my students for over 30 years. I would estimate that it has been cited by a ratio of over 100 to one over any other principle or maxim. Occasionally, one hears "Love your neighbor as yourself," (Mark 12:31) or "Do unto others as you would have others do on unto you" (Luke 6:31). Though over this period I have taught at a Jesuit university that is explicitly committed to social justice, I almost never hear such more radical Christian principles as "Inasmuch as you have done it to the least of these my brethren you have done it unto me" (Matthew 25:40). As was noted, Hardin cites the supposed Christian maxim of "being ones brother's keeper" (Genesis 4:9). However, this is not in fact a Christian moral injunction but rather Cain's evasive reply to God about his dead brother Abel's whereabouts in the ancient Hebrew myth of the first murder. There is great irony in Hardin's citation of this passage, for while "being another's keeper" is hardly the best way to describe disinterested love or care, Hardin's own rejection of responsibility to help those in need is echoed rather well in Cain's sarcastic retort.

While most students like the "teaching to fish" idea and often attribute it to Hardin himself when summarizing his position, he actually invokes it only to argue against it. In his view, it is the principle behind the "Green Revolution," which in his view has been a disaster. And, in fact, it *has* been a disaster in so far as the introduction of chemical-intensive monocrop agriculture that is at its core has hurt rather than helped the poor in whose name it is often defended. But he has no objection to the program's actual failures. According to his analysis, "'Miracle wheat' and 'miracle rice' are splendid technological achievements in the realm of plant genetics" (83). He fully approves of science working miracles. The problem for him only arises when the miracles are used, for example, to help needy human beings acquire more food to eat, and he fears that the Green Revolution may have had such a noxious effect. Not only does Hardin not want to give anyone a fish, he is not interested in allowing fish to remain where they might do harm, such as helping to keep the labor supply above the optimal level. The unrecognized principle behind his lifeboat world is "take a fish from a man and you can eat for a day, get a man to fish for you and give you the fish, and you can live on a rich lifeboat for the rest of your days."[6]

On Letting Indians Die

The brutality of Hardin's position becomes most evident when he comes to the topic of India, the country that has long aroused great horror in the neo-Malthusian imagination. He states that "the present population of India is 600 million, and it is increasing by 15 million per year," and that "every one of the net 15 million lives added each year stresses the Indian Environment more severely," concluding that *"every life saved this year in a poor country diminishes the quality of life for subsequent generations"* (84, emphasis in the original). What is most disturbing about this principle is what it clearly implies but discretely refrains from stating explicitly: "every life *lost*

43

this year in a poor country improves the quality of life for subsequent generations."

Hardin's ideology prevents him from following this somber reasoning to its logical conclusion. If saving lives in poor countries harms posterity, saving lives in rich countries in which each person consumes 30 times as much as a poor Indian can only be absolutely devastating to future generations. Allowing these heavy consumers of scarce resources to die, would, by Hardin's own standards, have highly beneficial long-term consequences. Yet, he raises no questions about the enormous amounts of money that are spent on such evils as saving the lives of heart patients, cancer victims, etc. in the developed world. He must realize that merely allowing infants in rich countries (any infants, but especially those from rich families) to die, rather than caring for them, would cut short highly damaging futures that would entail enormous consumption of resources and pollution of the environment. *Every death of an infant allowed to die in a rich country* would reduce the stress on the biosphere vastly more than the death of that poor person in India whom Hardin cautions us against saving. Nevertheless, Hardin, who prided himself on being a fearless iconoclast and "stalker of taboos," lacked the courage to track down such clear implications of his own deranged logic.[7]

We will not pursue such intriguing implications further. Instead, let us look at Hardin's central claims about famine in a country like India. Is there any truth in his contention that famine in such a country results from population stress on the resources of the country? The answer to this question emerges quite clearly from a source that Hardin would never think of investigating: the actual political, economic, and demographic history of India. An excellent presentation of the evidence offered by this history is found in Mike Davis's brilliant and powerful work, *Late Victorian Holocausts*. There, Davis traces in three fascinating and horrifying chapters the ways in which economic and political domination created the conditions for food scarcity and ultimately mass starvation in the subcontinent.[8]

It is a long and complicated story, but there are three essential moments: first, the forcible disruption of the traditional Indian subsistence economy; second, the use of law, policy, and brute force to make Indian labor completely subservient to the demands of imperial economic interests; and finally, when economic and political factors combined with climatic conditions to produce severe food scarcity, the refusal to allocate for purposes of famine relief the large food surpluses that existed either elsewhere in India or in the stricken areas themselves.

Davis cites Lord Lytton, the Viceroy of British India (1876-80), who, in the face of the Great Famine of 1876-78, which killed between six and ten million Indians, decreed that "there is to be no interference of any kind on the part of Government with the object of reducing the price of food,'" and "denounced 'humanitarian hysterics.'"[9] Expressing similar views during a debate on the famine, Finance Minister Sir Evelyn Baring, who was considered a progressive reformer among British colonial administrators, stated that "every benevolent attempt made to mitigate the effects of famine and defective sanitation serves but to enhance the evils resulting from overpopulation."[10] Hardin's warning about the evil of saving Indian lives reads a bit like latter-day plagiarism of Sir Evelyn's words.

Sir Richard Temple, Lieutenant-Governor of Bengal, takes the analysis one inevitable ideological step further, blaming the victims in the most contemptuous manner for their own suffering. Reacting to reports of high mortality rates, he remarks that "the infatuation of these poor people in respect to eating the bread of idleness; their dread of marching on command to any distance from home; their preference often for extreme privation rather than submission to even simple and reasonable orders, can be fully believed only by those who have seen or personally known these things."[11] He judges most of the victims to be, in fact, victims of their own irresponsibility, and predicted that few will "be inclined to grieve much for the fate which they brought upon themselves, and which terminated lives of idleness and too often of crime."[12] Such views are, of course, echoed in Hardin's claims that the roots of the crisis lie in the rapid "breeding" of the poor and their desire to live off the wealth of others, rather than solving their own problems.

As is typical of colonial agricultural policy globally, the British colonial regime undermined India's traditional subsistence economy for the sake of its imperial economic interests. Davis explains that "subsistence farming in many parts of the North Western Provinces had been recently converted into a captive export sector to stabilize British grain prices" and "most of the provinces' cruder grain stocks like millet were commercially exported to the famine districts in Bombay and Madras Presidencies, leaving local peasants with no hedge against drought. The profits from grain exports, meanwhile, were pocketed by richer zamindars, moneylenders and grain merchants—not the direct producers."[13] Thus, the peasants' own traditional "safety-net" was undermined so that they would be at the mercy (or mercilessness) of the imperial economy.

Famine upon famine was to come. It again raged from 1896 to 1897, during the reign of the second Lord Elgin, Viceroy from 1894 to 1899. The government conceded that 4.5 million died, but later estimates place the death toll at 12 to 16 million. It was to be followed shortly by another great famine of 1899-1902, under the rule of the subsequent Viceroy, Lord Curzon. An official report on the 1899-1902 famine found that "there was a surplus of grain in Bengal and Burma sufficient to compensate even such gigantic shortfalls in western and central India."[14] The report observed that it was a "regional deficiency of employment and income," rather than any scarcity of food in India as a whole, "that posed a mortal threat to so many millions."[15] At the same time that available food was denied to the famine victims, Lord Curzon moralized that "any Government which imperiled the financial position of India in the interests of prodigal philanthropy would be open to serious criticism; but any government which by indiscriminate alms-giving weakened the fiber and demoralized the self-reliance of the population, would be guilty of a public crime."[16]

Davis notes that in Rajputana almost a million people died, while "grain traders earned immense profits as they shifted rice and millet stocks from the countryside to the cities."[17] In the official famine report, a district officer gave the following familiar explanation of famine deaths in Gujarat: "The Gujarati is a soft man, unused to privation, accustomed to earn his good food easily."[18] As millions died in the midst of agricultural surpluses and exports, Lord Curzon could state that "there had never been a famine when the general mortality has been less, when the distress has been more amply or swiftly relieved."[19] How could the British public possibly accept such a description of imperially engineered mass starvation? The answer lies in large part in imperially engineered ideology and imagination. Some aid was in fact being distributed to what had continually been depicted as the lazy multitudes of the Subcontinent. The official view was certainly no more difficult to believe than is today's widely-held precept that the American empire is essentially over-generous to the impoverished, exploited debtor countries of the world. In fact, many of these countries get far less aid than Lord Curzon was willing to bestow on the starving masses of India.

The horrors of famine in India were only the most

brutal manifestation of a long, complex history of exploitation and immiseration. Davis notes that "only moneylenders, absentee landlords, urban merchants and a handful of indigenous industrialists seemed to have benefited consistently from India's renewed importance in world trade," while the result for peasants was pauperization.[20] He observes that many small farmers replaced millet production with cotton, even though cotton prices were declining and they had then to buy the grain with their proceeds. This seemingly irrational choice made sense only because land was scarce for small producers and cotton had a higher return per acre. Most small farmers had so little land that neither crop was adequate to provide subsistence. In addition, other areas that formerly produced subsistence crops such as millet switched to more profitable export grain crops such as wheat.[21]

While Hardin asserts on the basis of vague stories that a commons leads to collapse, Davis presents actual historical evidence that in India, as elsewhere, it was the destruction of the subsistence economy, and, indeed, the dissolution of the ancient commons that paved the way for disaster.

> Village economy in India, as elsewhere in monsoonal Asia, augmented crops and handicrafts with stores of free goods from common lands: dry grass for fodder, shrub grass for rope, wood and dung for fuel, dung, leaves, and forest debris for fertilizer, clay for plastering houses, and, above all, clean water. All classes utilized these common property resources, but for poorer households they constituted the very margin of survival.[22]

Davis observes that as late as 1870, the 20 percent of India that was forested remained as common land, but "by the end of the decade, [these lands] were completely enclosed by armed agents of the state."[23] The colonial administration stripped the peasants of much of their traditional subsistence safety net, and left them at the mercy of a brutal and morally blind system of economic exploitation.

In the context of the actual history of India, "carrying capacity" in any given locale took on a very precise meaning: the degree to which the continued existence of any given group of Indians was economically profitable for the Empire. This is the identity of Hardin's unnamed "something else" that might effect, and sometimes reduce, the "carrying capacity" of a given area: it consists of the vicissitudes of social domination.

The British Empire has passed into history, but the history of India today in the age of the highly developed global economy teaches many of the same lessons as did the colonial period. Arundhati Roy, in her essay "The Greater Common Good,"[24] explains very well the relationship between food resources and the condition of the poor in India. Roy notes that in 1995, though India's population had increased from the 600 million when Hardin wrote his article to 932 million, "the granaries were overflowing with 30 million tons of unsold grain."[25] Thus, Hardin was clearly wrong in his assumption that countries like India would not be able to increase food production more rapidly than population increased. Roy also observes that at the same time that such surpluses existed, 40% of the population was living below the poverty line, and the poorest of the poor were vulnerable to food scarcity, particularly in times of crisis. She notes that during the drought of 1996, people in Kalahandi (in Orissa) died of starvation, though not only was there a surplus of grain in India, but rice was being exported from Kalahandi itself.[26]

Roy points out the deep economic and political reasons for such a tragedy. Today, just as a century ago, the subsistence economy and small peasant farming are being destroyed in response to the demands of evolving global capitalism. Earlier, this took place in the context of the British Empire; it is occurring now in the context of the transnational corporate economy. In both cases, an alliance between the global centers of economic power and domestic elites has driven the processes of economic transformation. Roy shows how the dominant model of development led to massive dam-building projects that displaced enormous masses of the poor. Legions of the *adivasi*, or tribal peoples, were forced out as a result of the flooding of lands. Poorer farmers, who could not afford new capital-intensive methods of production based on large-scale irrigation were also dispossessed. As she states,

> Lands on which farmers traditionally grew crops that don't need a great deal of water (maize, millet, barley, and a whole range of pulses) suddenly yield water-guzzling cash crops—cotton, rice, soya bean, and the biggest guzzler of all (like those finned fifties cars), sugar-cane .... People stop growing things that they can afford to eat, and start growing things that they can only afford to sell. By linking themselves to the 'market' they lose control over their lives.[27]

The conclusion is absolutely clear. It has not been population increase or anything related to "carrying capacity" that has driven the poorest of the poor of India to the point of such a precarious existence, but rather the imposition of the dominant model of "maldevelopment," as Vandana Shiva calls it, and the destruction of the subsistence economy.[28]

Looking To India

Recently the limits of academic discussion of issues in global ethics have been expanded by the increasingly frequent inclusion of the human capabilities approach developed by Amartya Sen and Martha Nussbaum.[29] This is a promising development in so far as it helps shift discussion toward more complex substantive debates concerning the effects of practices and institutions. Increasing attention has been directed to Sen's well-known analysis of world population issues in which India plays an exemplary role.[30] However, contrary to that country's role in Hardin's account, it appears not as the bad example in a cautionary tale, but rather as the locus of a model for sane and humane solutions, and indeed as the possible source of inspiration for a new path in global development.

Why are so many so blind to any signs of hope that emanate from this land that is so emblematic of the global South? Sen is perhaps too discrete to write explicitly of "capitalist ideology" and "the racist imaginary," referring instead to certain "delusions," but his analysis points to the significance of both of these determinants. He notes that "[m]any Northerners fear being engulfed by people from Asia and Africa," a long-held sentiment that has prevailed in much of the West and certainly underlies the appeal of Hardin's analysis to citizens of affluent countries.[31] Sen observes that while the proportion of the world's people living on these continents has increased in recent history, projections for the year 2050 would only return them to the 78 percent of the world population that they constituted from 1650 to 1750, before the modern European population explosion and mass colonization took off.[32] Demographic shift is a much less significant dimension of the changing character of the world system than is the generalized economic and political shift away from the Eurocentric world of the modern period. The declining economic and political hegemony of European society forms a strong historical basis for this reactive racist imaginary, in which anxiety about the growth in the relative wealth and power of the non-European world is denied direct recognition and is instead ideologically biologized and channeled as fear of excessive reproductive growth. In view of such a state of the imaginary, a punitive reaction to population growth in poor countries has immediate appeal ("immediate" meaning mediated so powerfully by ideology that it appears powerfully self-evident).

Sen explains that if we exit the world of delusion

for that of demographic reality, we find that there are two approaches to attaining the goal of reducing population growth. One, which in an extreme and brutal form is found in Hardin's "lifeboat ethics," Sen calls the "override approach." It assumes that coercion, punishment, and negative contingencies of various types are necessary to influence reproductive behavior. It follows Hardin's dictum that "all persuasion takes place through coercion."[33] Sen says that according to such an approach, "the family's personal decisions are overridden by some agency outside the family."[34] He has in mind primarily policies such as those of China, in which benefits are withdrawn, fines are imposed, and harsh social pressure is exercised as means of punishing families for having more than the allotted number of children. However, Hardin's proposal that scarcity of food should discipline families and regimes into limiting reproduction also qualifies as such an "override" approach. Sen argues that such an approach, in producing immiseration, may not only be ineffectual, but even have "exactly the opposite effect on family planning than the one intended."[35]

Sen argues that the collaborative approach, which prioritizes the participation of families in decision-making and improvement of their lives, is not only the most just and humane policy but also the most effective one. Such an approach "relies not on legal or economic restrictions but on rational decisions of women and men, based on expanded choices and enhanced security, and encouraged by open dialogue and extensive public discussions."[36] Sen, along with many who have done careful research on population trends, has found that certain positive social variables correlate strongly with declines in fertility rates. These include expanded employment opportunities for women, improved standard of living, greater economic security, readily-available contraception and information on family planning, improved education (especially for women), improved health care; lower mortality rates (above all, infant mortality rates), and improved diet.[37]

Such research shows that empirical evidence leads to conclusions that are precisely the opposite of those of Hardin concerning the relationship between food security and fertility rates. Sen points out that

> Sub-Saharan Africa lags behind other developing regions in economic security, in health care, in life expectancy, in basic education, and in political and economic stability. It should be no great surprise that it lags behind in family planning as well.[38]

This region, which has the world's highest rates of population growth, is also a world leader in another area: food scarcity. Sen compares food production for two three-year periods a decade apart and finds that the largest increases in food production took place in the global South. More specifically, however, the greatest increases (as much as 22 percent per capita in Asia) were in regions where birth rates were declining, while Africa, the one continent in which high birth rates were persisting, actually experienced a 6 percent per capita *decline* in food production.[39]

It is noteworthy that Sen's paradigm case of the success of collaborative approaches comes from India, Hardin's prime example of a country that needed to be starved into demographic compliance. Sen compares China's coercive or "override" approach to the "collaborative" one that has prevailed in the state of Kerala in southwest India. He argues that "the roots of Kerala's success" lay in the place of women in society. He points out Kerala's 86 percent female literacy rate (compared to China's 68 percent) and the high level of participation by women in politics and the economy, and observes that

> the adverse reactions that have been observed in China, such as infant mortality, have not occurred in Kerala. The results have been striking. Kerala's

birth rate fell from 44 per thousand in the 1950's to
18 by 1991.[40]

Since Sen wrote this, the birth rate in Kerala has dropped
to 14.6 per thousand, lower than that of the U.S., and is
still falling.[41] Moreover, Kerala's declining fertility was
accomplished along with a low infant mortality rate. It
was only 16.5 per thousand births (as opposed to China's
31 per thousand) when Sen wrote, and it has now fallen
to 12 per thousand.[42]

Comparisons of Kerala and China make a strong
case for participatory, voluntary, "collaborative" methods, as opposed to authoritarian, coercive, "override"
policies. Sen points out that "despite China's one-child
policy and other coercive measures, its fertility rate seems
to have fallen much less sharply than those of Kerala and
Tamil Nadu."[43] Sen makes the important point that even
though China has been less successful through coercive
methods than Kerala has been through non-coercive one,
it would be invalid hastily to attribute even those results
that have been achieved in China to the use of these coercive factors. He notes that China has instituted many positive programs that create the conditions for voluntary
reduction of fertility rates. These include programs that
have "expanded education for women as well as men,
made health care more generally available, provided
more job opportunities for women, and stimulated rapid
economic growth."[44] Thus, as a result of these programs,
one would have expected a decline in fertility rates, even
in the absence of coercive measures. The relative importance of the various factors can only be determined
through comparative analysis.

Sen makes an excellent point concerning the costs
of just and humane development. He notes that some believe that needed innovations in education, health care
and other areas would be very expensive. However, in
reality such programs are very labor-intensive, and given

the relatively low price of labor in poor countries, the cost of highly effective, sustainable development programs can be very modest. Sen points out that "Kerala, India's star performer in expanding education and reducing both death rates and birth rates, is among the poorer Indian states."[45] Even today, the several thousand dollars that one American family might spend in a given year on a new big-screen TV, for example, might cover a year's operating expenses for a health clinic or community center in an Indian town or village.

Finally, it should be mentioned that while Sen does not stress this adequately, his analysis points clearly to the central place of the system of patriarchy and male dominance in perpetuating all the social, economic and demographic problems that have been discussed. As Mies and Shiva point out, many have assumed that until recent times a high level of "natural fertility" prevailed that was "checked only by biological factors," whereas, in fact, "women, in particular, knew and practiced methods of contraception and birth control."[46] The Malthusian conditions that Hardin depicts as the inevitable course of nature in "less developed" societies have been to a significant degree the result of the destruction of women's control of reproduction under the influence of patriarchal institutions. Since he is completely blind to the true nature of systems of social domination, Hardin is unable to imagine the possibility that greater decision-making power for women—that is, greater justice rather than greater punitiveness—could be a key element in confronting social crisis.[47]

Hardin's Sinking Ship

Hardin's "lifeboat ethics" commits the perennial fallacy of ideological thinking. It perpetuates the illusion that certain aspects or moments can be abstracted from the larger whole–the social historical whole and the natural historical whole–of which they are an insepa-rable part. More specifically, Hardin's position is a very extreme and rather crude version of the sort of view that Thomas Pogge dissects in his analysis of the clearly un-tenable but nevertheless widely accepted "Purely Domes-tic Poverty Thesis," in which the larger, systemic dimen-sions of poverty are consistently overlooked.[48] Hardin offers absolutely no explanation of why a crisis, even if it involves a food shortage, should be blamed specifically on "overpopulation" or "exceeding carrying capacity" within some limited geographical area. His argument is circular, since the nature of "crisis" is never investigated but rather merely defined as an event caused by popula-tion increasing beyond "carrying-capacity" (or failing to decrease to some optimal diminished "carrying-capaci-ty") within the boundaries of a given nation-state.

His alluringly deceptive lifeboat metaphor ab-stracts selected phenomena, we might say, both spatially, from the web of global interconnections between societ-ies, economies, cultures, and ecosystems, and temporally, from their mutual determination through the unfolding and interpenetrating processes of history. We leave the space-time of earthly geography and history and enter into the ideological moment. As a popular cliché goes these days, "It is what it is."[49] The problem is that it never merely "is what it is." For Hardin, lifeboats are somehow stocked with large quantities of "goodies." In his ideologi-cal imagination, it is as if the "goodies" all just sprouted up inside the lifeboats on which they are found. The last thing that we are allowed to think within the ideological dream world is that any these "goodies" could come from some-where *outside* those lifeboats, for example, from the exploi-tation of the labor of the poor of other countries or from the appropriation of these countries' natural resources.[50]

A reply to Hardin in *Bioscience* that appeared shortly after his original article in that journal summarizes very well some of the overwhelming evidence that Hardin's lifeboat world was a fantasy, and that the condition of the poor is neither a product of purely domestic conditions, nor the result of their own misguided choices:

> First, by colonization and actual wars of commerce, and through the international marketplace, rich nations have arranged an exchange of goods that has maintained and even increased the economic imbalance between rich and poor nations. Until recently we have taken or otherwise obtained cheap raw material from poor nations and sold them expensive manufactured goods that they cannot make themselves. In the United States, the structure of tariffs and internal subsidies discriminates selectively against poor nations. In poor countries, the concentration on cash crops rather than on food crops, a legacy of colonial times, is now actively encouraged by western multinational corporations . . . . Second, U.S. foreign policy, including foreign aid programs, has favored "pro-Western" regimes, many of which govern in the interests of a wealthy elite and some of which are savagely repressive.[51]

But in the world of ideology, it is always the victim who is to blame.[52] Hardin states that a severe food crisis is an "emergency"—that is, "something like an accident, which is correctly defined as *an event that is certain to happen, though with a low frequency*" (77, emphasis in the original). He observes that "a well-run organization prepares for everything that is certain, including accidents and emergencies" (77). He complains that unlike such organizations, "the vast majority of the governments of the world today have no such policy," because "they lack either the wisdom or the competence, or both" (78). To paraphrase Hardin's theory: "They're just not as smart as we are." This is the global version of a scenario we know very well from its domestic applications. Many a community has been devastated and degraded by capitalist exploitation and racist oppression, after which the administration of its hollow shell has been entrusted to minority-group politicians. The inevitable ideological judgment is that "they don't know how to run their own communities."

Thus, Hardin waxes philosophical as he laments the fact that "wise sovereigns seem not to exist in the poor world today," and that "far more difficult than the transfer of wealth from one country to another is the transfer of wisdom between sovereign powers or between generations" (78). Yes, we all know that it's hard to fit wisdom in a care package or a time capsule. But the real problem is that Hardin ignores the pertinent fact that many Third World rulers, far from lacking the profound wisdom of their First World colleagues, are just as wise when it comes to defending their mutual political and economic class interests to the detriment of the lives and welfare of the majority of their populations. For Hardin, the "sovereigns" who oversee the transfer of wealth and resources, including food, from poor to rich countries are wise if they happen to live in the rich country that receives the benefits, but foolish if they live in the poor country that suffers the consequences. Yet this process and the poverty and malnutrition that result from it are caused by the worldly-wise, cooperative efforts of both, on behalf of the sovereign self-interest of each.

It is not difficult to perceive beneath Hardin's judgments about the wisdom and prudence of the poor countries of the world the kind of visceral aversion that so typically accompanies binary ideological thinking. He notes with obvious satisfaction the fact that "Gregg (1955) likened the growth and spreading of humanity over the surface of the earth to the metastasis of cancer in the human body, wryly remarking that 'Cancerous growths demand food, but, as far as I know, they have never been cured by getting it.'"[53] The wry Mr. Gregg's idea of "feeding" or "curing" cancerous growths is obviously absurd,[54] but the analogy is still of interest. Presumably, if human beings are in general like cancerous growths, and if cancerous growths are malignancies that are best "starved" to death, then it would be a good thing to starve to death any given human being, rich or poor, whether through our action or our inaction. But Hardin is not intellectually consistent enough to propose any such generalized misanthropy. As mentioned above, he is barred absolutely from following his analysis to its logical conclusion when logic leads in a direction that contradicts ideology.

Given a world in which, as Hardin admits, all countries have in a crucial sense exceeded carrying-capacity, and in which some have exceeded it far more than others, its follows that the latter are more cancer-like than the others. However, because his ideology blocks such an analysis, Hardin is utterly incapable of conceiving of human beings who live in the rich, "developed" world as cancer-like, despite the fact that their ecocidal impact and his life-boatism should compel him to do so. Far from proposing that beneficent, forward-looking ways of starving the rich to death should be contrived, he is clearly concerned that anything that might threaten those on the rich lifeboats should *never* occur. As is so common in ideological thinking, there is a process of splitting in which a pervasive evil is condensed and concentrated in the other. The ideologically correct position is that we (the affluent) must think of certain other human beings (the poor) as equivalent to cancerous growths and treat them accordingly. Further, we must ignore anything about ourselves that would put us in the same position as they are. This turns out to be the "cash value" of Hardin's "lifeboat ethics."

Following the Common

Ideology, it might be added, often has a more literal "cash value." It is important therefore, in conclusion, to note the centrality of the question of *property* to Hardin's outlook. This is a question that is never posed explicitly in his argument, but which always lies just beneath the surface. In formulating his central argument against food aid, he explains that:

> the fundamental error of the sharing ethics is that it leads to the tragedy of the commons. Under a system of private property the man (or group of men) [sic] who own property recognize their responsibility to care for it, for if they don't they will eventually suffer. A farmer, for instance, if he is intelligent, will allow no more cattle in a pasture than its carrying capacity justifies. If he overloads the pasture, weeds take over, erosion sets in, and the owner loses in the long run (74).

One must wonder where Hardin thought he had found such a utopian world in which private agricultural property prevails and in which there is nevertheless little erosion and degradation of the soil. In the actual world of private agricultural property that is increasingly dominated by corporate agribusiness, a large proportion of all agricultural land has been severely degraded and soil erosion has become one of the most acute global environmental crises.[55]

Hardin rather astoundingly ignores entirely the problem of externalities and the fact that all around him there exists a world in which, according to conventional "laws" of economic rationality, property owners can (and as a matter of course often do) pass costs on to society and to the natural world, while appropriating to themselves the economic benefits. This dismal history goes back to the ancient Latifundia and beyond, but the classic case today is the deforestation of the Amazon basin, which has produced vast social disruptions and made the single largest contribution to the global biodiversity crisis, the Sixth Great Mass Extinction, the greatest ecological catastrophe facing the planet. As is well-known, enormous areas of rain forest are burned each year by powerful ranchers to add grazing land to their expansive domains. Within a dozen years or less, the biologically richest and most diverse ecosystems in the world are turned into degraded wastelands, after which they are abandoned for new areas in which the cycle of destruction is repeated. Though this cycle is entirely typical in the history of large private land exploitation, it would be difficult to find a single example of a historic commons in which even a small fraction of this catastrophic "ruin" has taken place. Once again, the ideological inversion of reality is striking, for the history of private property might much more accurately be called "the Tragedy of the Loss of the Commons."

Elinor Ostrom has been perhaps the most prominent figure in the contemporary revival of the idea of the commons. Ostrom and Harini Nagendra delineate the differences between a true commons and the system that Hardin describes, pointing out that he consistently confuses a type of resource with a property system. The ill-fated free-for-all that Hardin describes as "the commons" is in fact a collection of "common-pool resources," while the historic commons has been something quite different, "a common property regime."[56] They explain that Hardin's theory applies to "settings where resource users are alienated from one another or cannot communicate effectively," but it fails to apply to "settings where resource users are able to create and sustain their own agreements to avoid serious problems of overharvesting."[57] In other words, it fails to apply to a true commons.

Ostrom and Nagendra show that empirical research has led to a historically grounded understanding of conditions under which a community organizes itself to provide for the sustainability of resources. They list such conditions as that:

> rules must be generally known and understood, considered relatively legitimate, generally followed, and enforced;
>
> the boundary of the resource is easy to identify;

changes in the state of the resource can be monitored at a relatively low cost;

the rate of change in resource condition and in the socioeconomic and technological conditions of users remains moderate;

communities maintain frequent social interactions with each other that increase trust within the community;

outsiders can be relatively easily excluded from accessing the resource; and

rule infractions are monitored and sanctioned.[58]

Contrast this very specific, empirically-based account of how a successful commons operates to Hardin's impressionistic scenario in which he merely fantasizes what must occur within a "commons."

Hardin contends that "in a crowded world of less than perfect human beings—and we will never know any other—mutual ruin is inevitable in the commons. This is the core of the tragedy of the commons" (75). Once again, what is so striking about ideology is not that it is wrong about the nature of things. After all, it shares that quality with ordinary ignorance and stupidity, though it can certainly not be reduced to either of these. As was discovered long ago in dialectical critique, what is so astounding about ideology is how regularly it depicts the world as precisely the opposite of what it is in reality.[59] Hardin's depiction of the commons is a paradigm case of such ideological distortion. His "Lifeboat World" is founded on an ideology of scarcity and a psychology of fear, and fantasy must always conform to its own foundations. In such a world, we must think above all about how we can defend ourselves against malignant others who are a threat to our well-being and even our survival. We are thus forbidden to ask the most fundamental question that would lead us in the direction of a just and compassionate society: "How can we organize ourselves to care best for the needs of all?" In Hardin's ideological world, any concern for the needs of the most needy, any aspiration to practice global solidarity, is dismissed a priori as a path to "ruin in the commons."

Such a harsh and brutal logic is inescapable once one becomes trapped in the inverted world of ideology. However, in the real, historical world, "mutual ruin," in the form of social disintegration and global ecological catastrophe has resulted not from any supposed excesses of solidarity. Rather, it has followed from the ruthless exploitation of human labor, from the plundering of the natural world, and from the dissolution of the structures of care and cooperation that have historically been associated precisely with the commons. Solidarity and mutual aid within the commons are among the social forces that have done most to avert an increasingly catastrophic course of history. They also hold the greatest promise of helping us reverse this self-destructive path.

Notes

1. *Statistical Abstract of the United States: 1974* (Washington, D.C.: U.S. Bureau of the Census, 1974), pp. 785-786; *Statistical Abstract of the United States: 1976* (Washington, D.C.: U.S. Bureau of the Census, 1976), p. 838.

2. *Statistical Abstract of the United States: 1979* (Washington, D.C.: U.S. Bureau of the Census, 1979), p. 829; *Statistical Abstract of the United States: 1993* (Washington, D.C.: U.S. Bureau of the Census, 1993), p. 807.

3. Michael Kinsley, "The Intellectual Free Lunch," in *The New Yorker*, February 6, 1995, p. 4.

4. Organisation for Economic Co-operation and Development, "Aid Flows Top USD 100 Billion in 2005," *OECD Website*, April 4, 2006; online at http://www.oecd.org/officialdocuments/publicdisplayd ocumentpdf/?cote=PAC/COM/NEWS(2006)9&docLanguage=En.

5. David Roodman, An Index of Donor Performance, Center for Global Development, April 2004, online at http://www.globalissues.org/TradeRelated/Debt/USAid.asp.

6. For a good explanation of how ideology is embedded in the "Give a man a fish" cliché, see the brief presentation, "Ed Whitfield on why the 'teaching a man to fish' parable is a lie"; online at https://www.youtube.com/watch?v=fPcIumnhB8I. Ed Whitfield is the co-founder and co-managing director of the Fund for Democratic Communities (F4DC)

7. Though at least one of his followers falsely gave him credit for practicing what he preached. On September 14, 2003 Hardin and his wife Jane committed suicide. According to a tribute on the Garrett Hardin Society website, on that date, "two people decided to make a little more room on spaceship earth." [See Ed Maschke, "Tribute to Garrett Hardin: Making space in the lifeboat" at http://www.garretthardinsociety.org/tributes/tr_maschke_2003sep.html.] However, this statement only demonstrates how even Hardin's own death can be exploited misleadingly for the cause of neo-Malthusian bad faith. It was obvious that the Hardins did not sacrifice their own lives to provide more room on the planet for other life-forms. Though they practiced typical eco-gestures such as recycling, the brute facts are that they lived a total of 169 years of very high levels of material consumption, and that they produced a number of offspring that would, if extrapolated, double the number of First World over-consumers in a single generation. Their choice to die at very advanced ages was a calculated one, based on a decision concerning their own quality of life. As an obituary pointed out, "Dr. Hardin, who suffered from a heart disorder, and his wife, who had Lou Gehrig's disease, were members of End-of-Life Choices, formerly known as the Hemlock Society." See Stuart Lavietes, "Garrett Hardin, 88, Ecologist Who Warned About Excesses" New York Times, October 28, 2003; online at http://www.nytimes.com/2003/10/28/science/28HARD.html.

8. Mike Davis, Late Victorian Holocausts: El Niño Famines and the Making of the Third World (London and New York: Verso Books, 2002).

9. Ibid., p. 31.

10. Ibid., p. 32.

11. *Ibid.*, p. 41.

12. *Ibid.*, p. 41.

13. *Ibid.*, p. 51.

14. *Ibid.*, p. 161.

15. *Ibid.*, p. 161.

16. *Ibid.*, p. 162.

17. *Ibid.*, p. 168.

18. *Ibid.*, p. 172.

19. *Ibid.*, p. 173.

20. *Ibid.*, p. 312.

21. *Ibid.*, p. 316.

22. *Ibid.*, p. 326.

23. *Ibid.*, p. 327.

24. Arundhati Roy, "The Greater Common Good," April 1999; online at http://www.narmada.org/gcg/gcg.html. This essay later became half of her book *The Cost of Living* (New York: Modern Library, 1999), pp. 1-90.

25. *Ibid.*

26. *Ibid.* See Devinder Sharma, "The Kalahandi Syndrome: Starvation in Spite of Plenty"; online at http://www.mindfully.org/Food/Kalahandi-Syndrome-Sharma19apr02.htm.

27. *Ibid.*

28. Shiva introduced the concept over 25 years ago in the widely reprinted chapter on "Development, Ecology and Women" in her classic work *Staying Alive: Women, Ecology and Development* (London and Atlantic Highlands, NJ: Zed Books, 1989). There she says that "maldevelopment militates against . . . equality in diversity, and superimposes the ideologically constructed category of western technological man as a uniform measure of the worth of classes, cultures and genders" (p. 5).

29. This is not to ignore the problematic nature of the politics that accompanies the capabilities approach in Sen and Nussbaum. Denis O'Hearn has summarized very well the serious problems regarding Sen's concepts of democracy, markets, individualism and community, and above all, his lack of a theory of global capitalism in his brief article "Amartya Sen's Development as Freedom: Ten Years Later" in *Policy & Practice: A Development Education Review*, Vol. 8, Spring, pp. 9-15; online at http://www.developmenteducationreview.com/issue8-focus1?page=show. I have discussed similar problems in Nussbaum's work in "Capabilities Theory and the Limits of Liberal Justice. A Review Article on Martha Nussbaum's 'Frontiers of Justice'" in *Human Rights Review*, Volume 10, Issue 4 (2009), pp. 583–604.

30. Amartya Sen, "Population: Delusion and Reality," in *New York Review of Books*, Vol. 41, No. 15, September, 22, 1994, pp. 62-71, online at http://www.uwmc.uwc.edu/geography/malthus/sen_NYR.htm. Subsequent quotations from Sen's argument are taken from this article.

31. *Ibid.*

32. *Ibid.*

33. From "Garrett Hardin Quotations" selected by the Garrett Hardin Society. See http://www.garretthardinsociety.org/info/quotes.html.

34. Sen, "Population: Delusion and Reality."

35. *Ibid.*

36. *Ibid.*

37. On these factors, see Francis Moore Lappé, Joseph Collins and Peter Rosset, *World Hunger: Twelve Myths* (New York: Grove Press, 1998), Ch. 3 and Robert Engelman, *More: Population, Nature, and What Women Want* (Washington, DC: Island Press, 2008).

38. Sen, "Population: Delusion and Reality."

39. *Ibid.*

40. *Ibid.*

41. Official Government of Kerala website at http://www.kerala.

gov.in, updated on August 4, 2010.

42. *Ibid.*

43. Sen, "Population: Delusion and Reality."

44. *Ibid.*

45. *Ibid.*

46. Maria Mies and Vandana Shiva, *Ecofeminism* (London and Atlantic Highlands, NJ: Zed Books, 1993), pp. 286-287.

47. For a good survey of the evidence for the importance globally of reproductive choice for women, see Robert Engelman, *More: Population, Nature, and What Women Want.*

48. See his article "'Assisting' the Global Poor" in Deen K. Chatterjee, ed., *The Ethics of Assistance: Morality and the Distant Needy* (Cambridge: Cambridge University Press, 2004). A version of this article can be found on several web sites.

49. For a detailed analysis of this topic, see John Clark, "It Is What It Isn't! A Defense of Dialectic" *Review 31* (Jan. 5, 2014); online at http://review31.co.uk/essay/view/7/it-is-what-it-isn't-a-defence-of-the-dialectic.

50. Nor, of course, are we to think about the fact that in return for producing "goodies" for the affluent, the less privileged are rewarded with "badies," that is, the social ills such as poverty, debt, corruption, oppression, and environmental devastation that are imposed on them.

51. William W. Murdoch and Allan Oaten, "Population and Food: Metaphors and the Reality" in *Bioscience* 25, 1975, p. 562. See also "Who carries whom?" in Mies and Shiva, *Ecofeminism*, pp. 283-285.

52. We might even call it "blame the victim who is also the benefactor." In Hardin's depiction, women of the global South are seen as no more than a drain on the world's resources, while, as Maria Mies points out, "two-thirds of all labor in the world is done by women," and "a very large proportion of female labor in the Third World is engaged in production of goods for the market in the rich countries." *Patriarchy and Accumulation on a World Scale: Women in the International Division of Labor* (London and New York: Zed Books, 1998), p. 117.

53. Alan Gregg, "A Medical Aspect of the Population Problem," in *Science*, 121, May 1955, pp. 681-682.gths to which neo-Malthusian social theory can go in standing reality on its head. He notes "the marked inequalities of health, wealth, and function so conspicuous among the human beings in overpopulated countries" and speculates that "possibly man's invention of caste and social stratification may be viewed in part as a device to rationalize and control these same distressing discrepancies of health, wealth, and status that increase as the population increases." Social inequality is somehow generated directly by population increase, existing prior to class or caste relationships. Class and caste thus appear as a kind of superstructure built on the material base of population and its immediate effects. In the end, the caste system turns out to be, among other things, a means of coping with distress—in effect, "the heart of a heartless world" of population growth.

54. Pursuing this anthropomorphizing approach, one might imagine: "My cancerous growth has been particularly hungry lately," or "My cancerous growth has a doctor's appointment today."

55. As a widely-cited article summarizes, "Each year, 75 billion tons of topsoil are removed from the land by wind and water erosion, with most coming from agricultural land." David Pimentel, et al, "Environmental and Economic Costs of Soil Erosion and Conservation Benefits," in *Science*, vol. 267, no. 5201, February 1995, p. 1117.

56. Harini Nagendra and Elinor Ostrom, "Governing the commons in the new millennium: A diversity of institutions for natural resource management" in *Encyclopedia of Earth* (August 12, 2008); online at http://www.eoearth.org/view/article/51cbede67896bb 431f694988/

57. *Ibid.*

58. *Ibid.*

59. It should be noted that although ideology works in part as an unconscious mechanism it is also developed and propagated consciously and systematically. Mies observes that "the neo-Malthusian strategy of putting the blame for poverty and hunger in the colonized countries on the poor themselves was systematically developed by the pillars of corporate capitalism

and imperialism, first by the Rockefeller Foundation, the US State Department and the US Agency for International Development (AID), then by the World Bank." Mies, *Patriarchy and Accumulation on a World Scale*, p. 121.

Living on a Lifeboat
by Garrett Hardin

Susanne Langer (1942) has shown that it is probably impossible to approach an unsolved problem save through the door of metaphor. Later, attempting to meet the demands of rigor, we may achieve some success in cleansing theory of metaphor, though our success is limited if we are unable to avoid using common language, which is shot through and through with fossil metaphors. (I count no less than five in the preceding two sentences.)

Since metaphorical thinking is inescapable it is pointless merely to weep about our human limitations. We must learn to live with them, to understand them, and to control them. "All of us," said George Eliot in Middlemarch, "get our thoughts entangled in metaphors, and act fatally on the strength of them". To avoid unconscious suicide we are well advised to pit one metaphor against another. From the interplay of competitive metaphors, thoroughly developed, we may come closer to metaphor-free solutions to our problems.

No generation has viewed the problem of the survival of the human species as seriously as we have. Inevitably, we have entered this world of concern through the door of metaphor. Environmentalists have emphasized the image of the earth as a spaceship—Spaceship Earth. Kenneth Boulding (1966) is the principal architect of this metaphor. It is time, he says, that we replace the wasteful "cowboy economy" of the past with the frugal "spaceship economy" required for continued survival in the limited world we now see ours to be. The metaphor is notably useful in justifying pollution control measures.

Unfortunately, the image of a spaceship is also used to promote measures that are suicidal. One of these is a generous immigration policy, which is only a particular instance of a class of policies that are in error because they lead to the tragedy of the commons (Hardin 1968). These suicidal policies are attractive because they mesh with what we unthinkingly take to be the ideals of "the best people". What is missing in the idealistic view is an insistence that rights and responsibilities must go together. The "generous" attitude of all too many people results in asserting inalienable rights while ignoring or denying matching responsibilities.

For the metaphor of a spaceship to be correct, the aggregate of people on board would have to be under unitary sovereign control (Ophuls 1974). A true ship always has a captain. It is conceivable that a ship could be run by a committee. But it could not possibly survive if its course were determined by bickering tribes that claimed rights without responsibilities.

What about Spaceship Earth? It certainly has no captain, and no executive committee. The United Nations is a toothless tiger, because the signatories of its charter wanted it that way. The spaceship metaphor is used only to justify spaceship demands on common resources without acknowledging corresponding spaceship responsibilities.

An understandable fear of decisive action leads people to embrace "incrementalism"—moving toward reform by tiny stages. As we shall see, this strategy is counterproductive in the area discussed here if it means accepting rights before responsibilities. Where human survival is at stake, the acceptance of responsibilities is a precondition to the acceptance of rights, if the two cannot be introduced simultaneously.

Lifeboat Ethics

Before taking up certain substantive issues let us look at an alternative metaphor, that of a lifeboat. In developing some relevant examples the following numerical values are assumed. Approximately two-thirds of the world is desperately poor, and only one-third is comparatively rich. The people in poor countries have an average per capita GNP (Gross National Product) of about $200 per year, the rich, of about $3,000. (For the United States it is nearly $5,000 per year.) Metaphorically, each rich nation amounts to a lifeboat full of comparatively rich people. The poor of the world are in other, much more crowded, lifeboats. Continuously, so to speak, the poor fall out of their lifeboats and swim for a while in the water outside, hoping to be admitted to a rich lifeboat, or in some other way to benefit from the "goodies" on board. What should the passengers on a rich lifeboat do? This is the central problem of "the ethics of a lifeboat."

First we must acknowledge that each lifeboat is effectively limited in capacity. The land of every nation has a limited carrying capacity. The exact limit is a matter for argument, but the energy crunch is convincing more people every day that we have already exceeded the carrying capacity of the land. We have been living on "capital"—stored petroleum and coal—and soon we must live on income alone.

Let us look at only one lifeboat—ours. The ethical problem is the same for all, and is as follows. Here we sit, say 50 people in a lifeboat. To be generous, let us assume our boat has a capacity of 10 more, making 60. (This, however, is to violate the engineering principle of the "safety factor." A new plant disease or a bad change in the weather may decimate our population if we don't

72

preserve some excess capacity as a safety factor.)

The 50 of us in the lifeboat see a 100 others swimming in the water outside, asking for admission to the boat, or for handouts. How shall we respond to their calls? There are several possibilities.

One. We may be tempted to try to live by the Christian ideal of being "our brother's keeper," or by the Marxian ideal (Marx 1875) of "from each according to his abilities, to each according to his needs." Since the needs of all are the same, we take all the needy into our boat, making a total of 150 in a boat with a capacity of 60. The boat is swamped, and everyone drowns. Complete justice, complete catastrophe.

Two. Since the boat has an unused excess capacity of 10, we admit just 10 more to it. This has the disadvantage of getting rid of the safety factor, for which action we will sooner or later pay dearly. Moreover, *which* 10 do we let in? "First come, first served?" The best 10? The neediest 10? How do we *discriminate*? And what do we say to the 90 who are excluded?

Three. Admit no more to the boat and preserve the small safety factor. Survival of the people in the lifeboat is then possible (though we shall have to be on our guard against boarding parties).

The last solution is abhorrent to many people. It is unjust, they say. Let us grant that it is.

"I feel guilty about my good luck," say some. The reply to this is simple: *Get out and yield your place to others.* Such a selfless action might satisfy the conscience of those who are addicted to guilt but it would not change the ethics of the lifeboat. The needy person to whom a guilt-addict yields his place will not himself feel guilty about his sudden good luck. (If he did he would not climb aboard.) The net result of conscience-stricken people relinquishing their unjustly held positions is the elimination of their kind of conscience from the lifeboat. The lifeboat, as it were, purifies itself of guilt. The ethics of the lifeboat persist, unchanged by such momentary aberrations.

This then is the basic metaphor within which we must work out our solutions. Let us enrich the image step by step with substantive additions from the real world.

Reproduction

The harsh characteristics of lifeboat ethics are heightened by reproduction, particularly by reproductive differences. The people inside the lifeboats of the wealthy nations are doubling in numbers every 87 years; those outside are doubling every 35 years, on the average. And the relative difference in prosperity is becoming greater.

Let us, for a while, think primarily of the U.S. lifeboat. As of 1973, the United States had a population of 210 million people who were increasing by 0.8% per year, that is, doubling in number every 87 years.

Although the citizens of rich nations are outnumbered two to one by the poor, let us imagine an equal number of poor people outside our lifeboat—a mere 210 million poor people reproducing at a quite different rate. If we imagine these to be the combined populations of Colombia, Venezuela, Ecuador, Morocco, Thailand, Pakistan, and the Philippines, the average rate of increase of the people "outside" is a 3.3% per year. The doubling time of this population is 21 years.

Suppose that all these countries, and the United States, agreed to live by the Marxian ideal, "to each according to his needs," the ideal of most Christians as well. Needs, of course, are determined by population size, which is affected by reproduction. Every nation regards its rate of reproduction as a sovereign right. If our lifeboat were big enough in the beginning it might be possible to live *for a while* by Christian-Marxian ideals. *Might*.

Initially, in the model given, the ratio of non-Americans to Americans would be one to one. But consider what the ratio would be 87 years later. By this time Americans would have doubled to a population of 420 million. The other group (doubling every 21 years) would now have swollen to 3,540 million. Each American would have more than eight people to share with. How could the lifeboat possibly keep afloat?

All this involves extrapolation of current trends into the future and is consequently suspect. Trends may change. Granted, but the change will not necessarily be favorable. If—as seems likely—the rate of population increase falls faster in the ethnic group presently inside the lifeboat than it does among those now outside, the future will turn out to be even worse than mathematics predicts, and sharing will be even more suicidal.

Ruin in the Commons

The fundamental error of the sharing ethics is that it leads to the tragedy of the commons. Under a system of private property the man (or group of men) who own property recognize their responsibility to care for it, for if they don't they will eventually suffer. A farmer, for instance, if he is intelligent, will allow no more cattle in a pasture than its carrying capacity justifies. If he overloads the pasture, weeds take over, erosion sets in, and the owner loses in the long run.

But if a pasture is run as a commons open to all, the right of each to use it is not matched by an operational responsibility to take care of it. It is no use asking independent herdsmen in a commons to act responsibly, for they dare not. The considerate herdsman who refrains from overloading the commons suffers more than a selfish one who says his needs are greater. (As Leo Durocher says, "Nice guys finish last.") Christian-Marxian idealism is counterproductive. That it *sounds* nice is no excuse. With distribution systems, as with individual morality, good intentions are no substitute for good performance.

A social system is stable only if it is insensitive to errors. To the Christian-Marxian idealist a selfish person is a sort of "error." Prosperity in the system of the commons cannot survive errors. If *everyone* would only restrain himself, all would be well; but it takes *only one less than everyone* to ruin a system of voluntary restraint. In a crowded world of less than perfect human beings—and we will never know any other—mutual ruin is inevitable in the commons. This is the core of the tragedy of the commons.

One of the major tasks of education today is to create such an awareness of the dangers of the commons that people will be able to recognize its many varieties, however disguised. There is pollution of the air and water because these media are treated as commons. Further growth of population and growth in the per capita conversion of natural resources into pollutants require that the system of the commons be modified or abandoned in the disposal of "externalities."

The fish populations of the oceans are exploited as commons, and ruin lies ahead. No technological invention can prevent this fate: in fact, all improvements in the art of fishing merely hasten the day of complete ruin. Only the replacement of the system of the commons with a responsible system can save oceanic fisheries.

The management of western rangelands, though nominally rational, is in fact (under the steady pressure of cattle ranchers) often merely a government-sanctioned system of the commons, drifting toward ultimate ruin for both the rangelands and the residual enterprisers.

World Food Banks

In the international arena we have recently heard a proposal to create a new commons, namely an international depository of food reserves to which nations will contribute according to their abilities, and from which nations may draw according to their needs. Nobel laureate Norman Borlaug has lent the prestige of his name to this proposal.

A world food bank appeals powerfully to our humanitarian impulses. We remember John Donne's celebrated line, "Any man's death diminishes me." But before we rush out to see for whom the bell tolls, let us recognize where the greatest political push for international granaries comes from, lest we be disillusioned later. Our experience with Public Law 480 clearly reveals the answer. This was the law that moved billions of dollars worth of U.S. grain to food-short, population-long countries during the past two decades. When P. L. 480 first came into being, a headline in the business magazine *Forbes* (Paddock and Paddock 1970) revealed the power behind it: "Feeding the World's Hungry Millions: How It Will Mean Billions for U.S. Business."

And indeed it did. In the years 1960 to 1970 a total of $7.9 billion was spent on the "Food for Peace" program, as P. L. 480 was called. During the years 1948 to 1970 an additional $49.9 billion were extracted from American taxpayers to pay for other economic aid programs, some of which went for food and food-producing machinery. (This figure does *not* include military aid.) That P. L. 480 was a give-away program was concealed. Recipient countries went through the motions of paying for P. L. 480 food—with IOUs. In December 1973 the charade was brought to an end as far as India was concerned when the United States "forgave" India's $3.2 billion debt (Anonymous 1974). Public announcement of the cancellation of the debt was delayed for two months; one wonders why.

"Famine—1974!" (Paddock and Paddock 1970) is one of the few publications that points out the commercial roots of this humanitarian attempt. Though all U.S. taxpayers lost by P. L. 480, special interest groups gained handsomely. Farmers benefited because they were not asked to contribute the grain—it was bought from them by the taxpayers. Besides the direct benefit there was the indirect effect of increasing demand and thus raising prices of farm products generally. The manufacturers of farm machinery, fertilizers, and pesticides benefited by the farmers' extra efforts to grow more food. Grain elevators profited from storing the grain for varying lengths of time. Railroads made money hauling it to port, and shipping lines by carrying it overseas. Moreover, once the machinery for P. L. 480 was established, an immense bureaucracy had a vested interest in its continuance regardless of its merits.

Very little was ever heard of these selfish interests when P. L. 480 was defended in public. The emphasis was always on its humanitarian effects. The combination of multiple and relatively silent selfish interests with highly vocal humanitarian apologists constitutes a powerful lobby for extracting money from taxpayers. Foreign aid has become a habit that can apparently survive in the absence of any known justification. A news commentator in a weekly magazine (Lansner 1974), after exhaustively going over all the conventional arguments for foreign aid—self-interest, social justice, political advantage, and charity—and concluding that none of the known arguments really held water, concluded: "So the search continues for some logically compelling reasons for giving aid ...". In other words, *Act now, Justify later*—if ever. (Apparently a quarter of a century is too short a time to find the justification for expending several billion dollars yearly.)

The search for a rational justification can be short-circuited by interjecting the word "emergency." Borlaug uses this word. We need to look sharply at it. What is an "emergency?" It is surely something like an accident, which is correctly defined as *an event that is certain to happen, though with a low frequency* (Hardin 1972a). A well-run organization prepares for everything that is certain, including accidents and emergencies. It budgets for them. It saves for them. It expects them—and mature decision-

78

makers do not waste time complaining about accidents when they occur.

What happens if some organizations budget for emergencies and other do not? If each organization is solely responsible for its own well-being, poorly managed ones will suffer. But they should be able to learn from experience. They have a chance to mend their ways and learn to budget for infrequent but certain emergencies. The weather, for instance, always varies and periodic crop failures are certain. A wise and competent government saves out of the production of the good years in anticipation of bad years that are sure to come.

This is not a new idea. The Bible tells us that Joseph taught this policy to Pharaoh in Egypt more than two thousand years ago. Yet it is literally true that the vast majority of the governments of the world today have no such policy. They lack either the wisdom or the competence, or both. Far more difficult than the transfer of wealth from one country to another is the transfer of wisdom between sovereign powers or between generations.

"But it isn't their fault! How can we blame the poor people who are caught in an emergency? Why must we punish them?" The concepts of blame and punishment are irrelevant. The question is, what are the operational consequences of establishing a world food bank? If it is open to every country every time a need develops, slovenly rulers will not be motivated to take Joseph's advice. Why should they? Others will bail them out whenever they are in trouble.

Some countries will make deposits in the world food bank and others will withdraw from it: There will be almost no overlap. Calling such a depository-transfer unit a "bank" is stretching the metaphor of *bank* beyond its elastic limits. The proposers, of course, never call attention to the metaphorical nature of the word they use.

The Ratchet Effect

An "international food bank" is really, then, not a true bank but a disguised one-way transfer device for moving wealth from rich countries to poor. In the absence of such a bank, in a world inhabited by individually responsible sovereign nations, the population of each nation would repeatedly go through a cycle of the sort shown in Figure 1. P_2 is greater than P_1, either in absolute numbers or because a deterioration of the food supply has removed the safety factor and produced a dangerously low ratio of resources to population. P_2 may be said to represent a state of overpopulation, which becomes obvious upon the appearance of an "accident," e.g., a crop failure. If the "emergency" is not met by outside help, the population drops back to the "normal" level—the "carrying capacity" of the environment—or even below. In the absence of population control by a sovereign, sooner or later the population grows to P_2 again and the cycle repeats. The long-term population curve (Hardin 1966) is an irregularly fluctuating one, equilibrating more or less about the carrying capacity.

A demographic cycle of this sort obviously involves great suffering in the restrictive phase, but such a cycle is normal to any independent country with inadequate population control. The third century theologian Tertullian (Hardin 1969a) expressed what must have been the recognition of many wise men when he wrote: "The scourges of pestilence, famine, wars, and earthquakes have come to be regarded as a blessing to overcrowded nations, since they serve to prune away the luxuriant growth of the human race."

Only under a strong and farsighted sovereign—which theoretically could be the people themselves, democratically organized—can a population equilibrate at some set point below the carrying capacity, thus avoiding the pains normally caused by periodic and un-

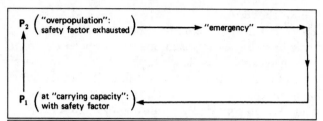

Figure 1. The population cycle of a nation that has no effective, conscious population control, and which receives no aid from the outside. P_2 is greater than P_1.

avoidable disasters. For this happy state to be achieved it is necessary that those in power be able to contemplate with equanimity the "waste" of surplus food in times of bountiful harvests. It is essential that those in power resist the temptation to convert extra food into extra babies. On the public relations level it is necessary that the phrase "surplus food" be replaced by "safety factor."

But wise sovereigns seem not to exist in the poor world today. The most anguishing problems are created by poor countries that are governed by rulers insufficiently wise and powerful. If such countries can draw on

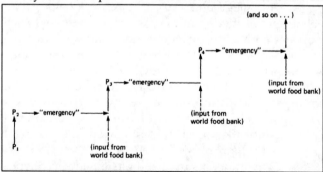

Figure 2. The population escalator. Note that in- put from a world food bank acts like the pawl of a ratchet, preserving the normal population cycle shown in Figure 1 from being completed. P_{n+1} is greater than P_n, and the absolute magnitude of the "emergencies" escalates. Ultimately the entire system crashes. The crash is not shown, and few can imagine it.

a world food bank in times of "emergency," the population *cycle* of Figure 1 will be replaced by the population *escalator* of Figure 2. The input of food from a food bank acts as the pawl of a ratchet, preventing the population from retracing its steps to a lower level. Reproduction pushes the population upward, inputs from the World Bank prevent its moving downward. Population size escalates, as does the absolute magnitude of "accidents" and "emergencies." The process is brought to an end only by the total collapse of the whole system, producing a catastrophe of scarcely imaginable proportions.

Such are the implications of the well-meant sharing of food in a world of irresponsible reproduction.

I think we need a new word for systems like this. The adjective "melioristic" is applied to systems that produce continual improvement; the English word is derived from the Latin *meliorare*, to become or make better. Parallel with this it would be useful to bring in the word *pejoristic* (from the Latin *pejorare*, to become or make worse.) This word can be applied to those systems which, by their very nature, can be relied upon to make matters worse. A world food bank coupled with sovereign state irresponsibility in reproduction is an example of a pejoristic system.

This pejoristic system creates an unacknowledged commons. People have more motivation to draw from than to add to the common store. The license to make such withdrawals diminishes whatever motivation poor countries might otherwise have to control their populations. Under the guidance of this ratchet, wealth can be steadily moved in one direction only, from the slowly-breeding rich to the rapidly-breeding poor, the process finally coming to a halt only when all countries are equally and miserably poor.

All this is terribly obvious once we are acutely aware of the pervasiveness and danger of the commons. But many people still lack this awareness and the euphoria of the "benign demographic transition" (Hardin 1973) interferes with the realistic appraisal of pejoristic mechanisms. As concerns public policy, the deductions drawn from the benign demographic transition are these:

1) If the per capita GNP rises the birth rate will fall; hence, the rate of population increase will fall, ultimately producing ZPG (Zero Population Growth).

2) The long-term trend all over the world (including the poor countries) is of a rising per capita GNP (for which no limit is seen).

3) Therefore, all political interference in population matters is unnecessary; all we need to do is foster economic "development"—*note the metaphor*—and population problems will solve themselves.

Those who believe in the benign demographic transition dismiss the pejoristic mechanism of Figure 2 in the belief that each input of food from the world outside fosters development within a poor country thus resulting in a drop in the rate of population increase. Foreign aid has proceeded on this assumption for more than two decades. Unfortunately, it has produced no indubitable instance of the asserted effect. It has, however, produced a library of excuses. The air is filled with plaintive calls for more massive foreign aid appropriations so that the hypothetical melioristic process can get started.

The doctrine of demographic laissez-faire implicit in the hypothesis of the benign demographic transition is immensely attractive. Unfortunately there is more evidence against the melioristic system than there is for it (Davis 1963). On the historical side there are many counter examples. The rise in per capita GNP in France and Ireland during the past century has been accompanied by a rise in population growth. In the 20 years following the Second World War the same positive correlation was noted almost everywhere in the world. Never in world history before 1950 did the worldwide population growth reach 1% per annum. Now the average population growth is over 2% and shows no signs of slackening.

On the theoretical side, the denial of the pejoristic scheme of Figure 2 probably springs from the hidden acceptance of the "cowboy economy" that Boulding castigated. Those who recognize the limitations of a spaceship, if they are unable to achieve population control at a safe and comfortable level, accept the necessity of the corrective feedback of the population cycle shown in Figure 1. No one who knew in his bones that he was living on a true spaceship would countenance political support of the population escalator shown in Figure 2.

Eco-Destruction Via the Green Revolution

The demoralizing effect of charity on the recipient has long been known. "Give a man a fish and he will eat for a day; teach him how to fish and he will eat for the rest of his days." So runs an ancient Chinese proverb. Acting on this advice the Rockefeller and Ford Foundations have financed a multipronged program for improving agriculture in the hungry nations. The result, known as the "Green Revolution," has been quite remarkable. "Miracle wheat" and "miracle rice" are splendid technological achievements in the realm of plant genetics.

Observant critics have shown how much harm we wealthy nations have already done to poor nations through our well-intentioned but misguided attempts to help them.

Whether or not the Green Revolution can increase food production is doubtful (Harris 1972, Paddock 1970, Wilkes 1972), but in any event not particularly important. What is missing in this great and well-meaning humanitarian effort is a firm grasp of fundamentals. Considering the importance of the Rockefeller Foundation in this effort it is ironic that the late Alan Gregg, a much-respected vice-president of the Foundation, strongly expressed his doubts of the wisdom of all attempts to increase food production some two decades ago. (This was before Borlaug's work—supported by Rockefeller—had resulted in the development of "miracle wheat"). Gregg (1955) likened the growth and spreading of humanity over the surface of the earth to the metastasis of cancer in the human body, wryly remarking that "Cancerous growths demand food; but, as far as I know, they have never been cured by getting it."

"Man does not live by bread alone"—the scriptural statement has a rich meaning even in the material realm. Every human being born constitutes a draft on all aspects of the environment—food, air, water, unspoiled scenery, occasional and optional solitude, beaches, contact with wild animals, fishing, hunting—the list is long and incompletely known. Food can, perhaps, be significantly increased: but what about clean beaches, unspoiled forests, and solitude? If we satisfy the need for food in a growing population we necessarily decrease the supply of other goods, and thereby increase the difficulty of equitably allocating scarce goods (Hardin 1969b, 1972b).

The present population of India is 600 million, and it is increasing by 15 million per year. The environmental load of this population is already great. The forests of India are only a small fraction of what they were three centuries ago. Soil erosion, floods, and the psychological costs of crowding are serious. Every one of the net 15 million lives added each year stresses the Indian Environment more severely. *Every life saved this year in a poor country diminishes the quality of life for subsequent generations.*

Observant critics have shown how much harm we wealthy nations have already done to poor nations through our well-intentioned but misguided attempts to help them (Paddock and Paddock 1973). Particularly reprehensible is our failure to carry out post-audits of these attempts (Farvar and Milton 1972). Thus have we

85

shielded our tender consciences from knowledge of the harm we have done. Must we Americans continue to fail to monitor the consequences of our external "do-gooding?" If, for instance, we thoughtlessly make it possible for the present 600 million Indians to swell to 1,200 million by the year 2001—as their present growth rate promises—will posterity in India thank *us* for facilitating an even greater destruction of *their* Environment? Are good intentions ever a sufficient excuse for bad consequences?

Immigration Creates A Commons

I come now to the final example of a commons in action, one for which the public is least prepared for rational discussion. The topic is at present enveloped by a great silence which reminds me of a comment made by Sherlock Holmes in A. Conan Doyle's story "Silver Blaze." Inspector Gregory had asked, "Is there any point to which you would wish to draw my attention?" To this Holmes responded:

> "To the curious incident of the dog in the nighttime."
> "The dog did nothing in the nighttime," said the Inspector.
> "That was the curious incident," remarked Sherlock Holmes

By asking himself what would repress the normal barking instinct of a watchdog, Holmes realized that it must be the dog's recognition of his master as the criminal trespasser. In a similar way we should ask ourselves what repression keeps us from discussing something as important as immigration.

It cannot be that immigration is numerically of no consequence. Our government acknowledges a *net* inflow of 400,000 a year. Hard data are understandably lacking on the extent of illegal entries, but a not implausible figure is 600,000 per year (Buchanan 1973). The natural increase of the resident population is now about 1.7 million per year. This means that the yearly gain from immigration is at least 19%, and may be 37%, of the total increase. It is quite conceivable that educational campaigns like that of Zero Population Growth, Inc., coupled with adverse social and economic factors—inflation, housing shortage, depression, and loss of confidence in national leaders— may lower the fertility of American women to a point at which all of the yearly increase in population would be accounted for by immigration. Should we not at least ask if that is what we want? How curious it is that we so seldom discuss immigration these days!

Curious, but understandable—as one finds out the moment he publicly questions the wisdom of the status quo in immigration. He who does so is promptly charged with *isolationism, bigotry, prejudice, ethnocentrism, chauvinism*, and *selfishness*. These are hard accusations to bear. It is pleasanter to talk about other matters, leaving immigration policy to wallow in the cross-currents of special interests that take no account of the good of the whole—*or of the interests of posterity*.

We Americans have a bad conscience because of things we said in the past about immigrants. Two generations ago the popular press was rife with references to *Dagos, Wops, Polacks, Japs, Chinks*, and *Krauts*—all pejorative terms which failed to acknowledge our indebtedness to Goya, Leonardo, Copernicus, Hiroshige, Confucius, and Bach. Because the implied inferiority of foreigners was *then* the justification for keeping them out, it is *now* thoughtlessly assumed that restrictive policies can only be based on the assumption of immigrant inferiority. *This is not so.*

Existing immigration laws exclude idiots and known criminals; future laws will almost certainly continue this policy. But should we also consider the quality of the average immigrant, as compared with the quality of the average resident? Perhaps we should, perhaps we shouldn't. (What is "quality" anyway?) But the quality issue is not our concern here.

From this point on, *it will be assumed that immigrants and native-born citizens are of exactly equal quality,* however quality may be defined. The focus is only on quantity. The conclusions reached depend on nothing else, so all charges of ethnocentrism are irrelevant.

World food banks move food to the people, thus facilitating the exhaustion of the Environment of the poor. By contrast, unrestricted immigration moves people to the food, thus speeding up the destruction of the Environment in rich countries. Why poor people should want to make this transfer is no mystery; but why should rich hosts encourage it? This transfer, like the reverse one, is supported by both selfish interests and humanitarian impulses.

The principal selfish interest in unimpeded immigration is easy to identify: It is the interest of the employers of cheap labor, particularly that needed for degrading jobs. We have been deceived about the forces of history by the lines of Emma Lazarus inscribed on the Statue of Liberty:

> *Give me your tired, your poor*
> *Your huddled masses*
> *yearning to breathe free,*
> *The wretched refuse of your*
> *teeming shore,*
> *Send these, the homeless,*
> *tempest-tossed, to me:*
> *I lift my lamp beside the*
> *golden door.*

The image is one of an infinitely generous earth-mother, passively opening her arms to hordes of immigrants who come here on their own initiative. Such an image may have been adequate for the early days of colonization, but by the time these lines were written (1886) the force for immigration was largely manufactured inside our own borders by factory and mine owners who sought cheap labor not to be found among laborers already here. One group of foreigners after another was thus enticed into the United States to work at wretched jobs for wretched wages.

At present, it is largely the Mexicans who are being so exploited. It is particularly to the advantage of certain employers that there be many illegal immigrants. Illegal immigrant workers dare not complain about their working conditions for fear of being repatriated. Their presence reduces the bargaining power of all Mexican-American laborers. Cesar Chavez has repeatedly pleaded with congressional committees to close the doors to more Mexicans so that those here can negotiate effectively for higher wages and decent working conditions. Chavez understands the ethics of a lifeboat.

The interests of the employers of cheap labor are well served by the silence of the intelligentsia of the country. WASPS—White Anglo-Saxon Protestants—are particularly reluctant to call for a closing of the doors to immigration for fear of being called ethnocentric bigots. It was, therefore, an occasion of pure delight for this particular WASP to be present at a meeting when the points he would like to have made were made better by a non-WASP, speaking to other non-WASPS. It was in Hawaii, and most of the people in the room were second-level Hawaiian officials of Japanese ancestry. All Hawaiians are keenly aware of the limits of their Environment, and the speaker had asked how it might be practically and constitutionally possible to close the doors to more immigrants to the islands. (To Hawaiians, immigrants from the other

49 states are as much of a threat as those from other nations. There is only so much room in the islands, and the islanders know it. Sophistical arguments that imply otherwise do not impress them.)

Yet the Japanese-Americans of Hawaii have active ties with the land of their origin. This point was raised by a Japanese-American member of the audience who asked the Japanese-American speaker: "But how can we shut the doors now? We have many friends and relations in Japan that we'd like to bring to Hawaii some day so that they can enjoy this land."

The speaker smiled sympathetically and responded slowly: Yes, but we have children now and someday we'll have grandchildren. We can bring more people here from Japan only by giving away some of the land that we hope to pass on to our grandchildren some day. What right do we have to do that?

To be generous with one's own possessions is one thing; to be generous with posterity's is quite another. This, I think, is the point that must be gotten across to those who would, from a commendable love of distributive justice, institute a ruinous system of the commons, either in the form of a world food bank or that of unrestricted immigration. Since every speaker is a member of some ethnic group it is always possible to charge him with ethnocentrism. But even after purging an argument of ethnocentrism the rejection of the commons is still valid and necessary if we are to save at least some parts of the world from Environmental ruin. Is it not desirable that at least some of the grandchildren of people now living should have a decent place in which to live?

The Asymmetry of Door-Shutting

We must now answer this telling point: "How can you justify slamming the door once you're inside?" You say that immigrants should be kept out. But aren't we all

90

immigrants, or the descendants of immigrants? Since we refuse to leave, must we not, as a matter of justice and symmetry, admit all others?"

It is literally true that we Americans of non-Indian ancestry are the descendants of thieves. Should we not, then, "give back" the land to the Indians; that is, give it to the now-living Americans of Indian ancestry? As an exercise in pure logic I see no way to reject this proposal. Yet I am unwilling to live by it; and I know no one who is. Our reluctance to embrace pure justice may spring from pure selfishness. On the other hand, it may arise from an unspoken recognition of consequences that have not yet been clearly spelled out.

Suppose, becoming intoxicated with pure justice, we "Anglos" should decide to turn our land over to the Indians. Since all our other wealth has also been derived from the land, we would have to give that to the Indians, too. Then what would we non-Indians do? Where would we go? There is no open land in the world on which men without capital can make their living (and not much unoccupied land on which men with capital can, either). Where would 209 million putatively justice-loving, non-Indian, Americans go? Most of them—in the persons of their ancestors—came from Europe, but they wouldn't be welcomed back there. Anyway, Europeans have no better title to their land than we to ours. They also would have to give up their homes. (But to whom? And where would *they* go?)

Clearly, the concept of pure justice produces an infinite regress. The law long ago invented statutes of limitations to justify the rejection of pure justice, in the interest of preventing massive disorder. The law zealously defends property rights—but only *recent* property rights. It is as though the physical principle of exponential decay applies to property rights. Drawing a line in time may be unjust, but any other action is practically worse.

We are all the descendants of thieves, and the world's resources are inequitably distributed, but we must begin the journey to tomorrow from the point where we are today. We cannot remake the past. We cannot, without violent disorder and suffering, give land and resources back to the "original" owners—who are dead anyway.

We cannot safely divide the wealth equitably among all present peoples, so long as people reproduce at different rates, because to do so would guarantee that our grandchildren—everyone's grandchildren—would have only a ruined world to inhabit.

Must Exclusion Be Absolute?

To show the logical structure of the immigration problem I have ignored many factors that would enter into real decisions made in a real world. No matter how convincing the logic may be it is probable that we would want, from time to time, to admit a few people from the outside to our lifeboat. Political refugees in particular are likely to cause us to make exceptions: We remember the Jewish refugees from Germany after 1933, and the Hungarian refugees after 1956. Moreover, the interests of national defense, broadly conceived, could justify admitting many men and women of unusual talents, whether refugees or not. (This raises the quality issue, which is not the subject of this essay.)

Such exceptions threaten to create runaway population growth inside the lifeboat, i.e., the receiving country. However, the threat can be neutralized by a population policy that includes immigration. An effective policy is one of flexible control.

Suppose, for example, that the nation has achieved a stable condition of ZPG, which (say) permits 1.5 million births yearly. We must suppose that an acceptable system of allocating birthrights to potential parents is in effect. Now suppose that an inhumane regime in some other part of the world creates a horde of refugees, and that there is a widespread desire to admit some to our country. At the same time, we do not want to sabotage our population control system. Clearly, the rational path to pursue is the following: If we decide to admit 100,000 refugees this year we should compensate for this by reducing the allocation of birth rights in the following year by a similar amount, that is downward to a total of 1.4 million. In that way we could achieve both humanitarian and population control goals. (And the refugees would have to accept the population controls of the society that admits them. It is not inconceivable that they might be given proportionately fewer rights than the native population.)

In a democracy, the admission of immigrants should properly be voted on. But, by whom? It is not obvious. The usual rule of a democracy is votes for all. But it can be questioned whether a universal franchise is the most just one in a case of this sort. Whatever benefits there are in the admission of immigrants presumably accrue to everyone. But the costs would be seen as falling most heavily on potential parents, some of whom would have to postpone or forego having their (next) child because of the influx of immigrants. The double question *Who benefits? Who pays?* suggests that a restriction of the usual democratic franchise would be appropriate and just in this case. Would our particular quasi-democratic form of government be flexible enough to institute such a novelty? If not, the majority might, out of humanitarian motives, impose an unacceptable burden (the foregoing of parenthood) on a minority, thus producing political instability.

Plainly many new problems will arise when we consciously face the immigration question and seek rational answers. No workable answers can be found if we ignore population problems. And—if the argument of this essay is correct—so long as there is no true world government to control reproduction everywhere it is impossible to survive in dignity if we are to be guided by Spaceship ethics. Without a world government that is sovereign in reproductive matters mankind lives, in fact, on a number of sovereign lifeboats. For the foreseeable future survival demands that we govern our actions by the ethics of a lifeboat. Posterity will be ill served if we do not.

References

Anonymous. 1974. *Wall Street Journal*, 19 Feb.

Borlaug, N. 1973. "Civilization's Future: A Call for International Granaries." *Bull. At. Sci.* 29:7-15.

Boulding, K. 1966. "The Economics of the Coming Spaceship Earth." *In*, H. Jarrett, ed., Environmental Quality in a Growing Economy. Johns Hopkins Press, Baltimore.

Buchanan, W. 1973. "Immigration Statistics." *Equilibrium* 1(3):16-19.

Davis, K. 1963. "Population." *Sci. Amer.* 209(3): 62-71.

Farvar, M. T., and J. P. Milton. 1972. The Careless Technology. Natural History Press, Garden City, N.Y.

Gregg, A. 1955. "A Medical Aspect of the Population Problem." *Science* 121:681-682.

Hardin, G. 1966. Chapter 9 *in* Biology: Its Principles and Implications, 2nd ed. Freeman, San Francisco.

—1968. "The Tragedy of the Commons," *Science* 162:1243-1248.

—1969a Page 18 *in* Population, Evolution and Birth Control, 2nd ed. Freeman, San Francisco.

—1969b. "The Economics of Wilderness." *Nat. Hist.* 78(6):20-27.

—1972a. Pages 81-82 *in* Exploring New Ethics for Survival: The Voyage of the Spaceship Beagle. Viking, N.Y.

—1972b. "Preserving Quality on Spaceship Earth." *In* J. B. Trefethen, ed. Transactions of the Thirty-Seventh North American Wildlife and Natural Resources Conference, Wildlife Management Institute, Washington, DC.

—1973. Chapter 23 *in* Stalking the Wild Taboo. Kaufmann, Los Altos, CA.

Harris, M. 1972. "How Green the Revolution?" *Nat. Hist.* 81(3):28-30.

Langer, S. K. 1942. Philosophy *in* a New Key. Harvard University Press, Cambridge.

Lansner, K. 1974. "Should Foreign Aid Begin at Home?" *Newsweek*, 11 Feb., p.32.

Marx, K. 1875. "Critique of the Gotha Program." Page 388 *in* R. C. Tucker, ed. The Marx-Engels Reader. Norton, N.Y., 1972.

Ophuls, W. 1974. "The Scarcity Society." *Harpers* 243(1487):47-52.

Paddock, W. C. 1970. "How Green Is the Green Revolution?" *BioScience* 20:897-902.

Paddock, W., and E. Paddock. 1973. We Don't Know How. Iowa State University Press, Ames, Iowa.

Paddock, W. and P. Paddock. 1967. Famine -1975! Little, Brown, Boston.

Wilkes, H. G. 1972. "The Green Revolution." *Environment* 14 (8):32-39.

Global Fertility Rates (2014)[1]

1. Niger	6.89	22. Congo, Dem. Rep. of the	4.80
2. Mali	6.16	23. Congo, Rep. of the	4.73
3. Burundi	6.14	24. Chad	4.68
4. Somalia	6.08	25. Sao Tome and Principe	4.67
5. Uganda	5.97	26. Equatorial Guinea	4.66
6. Burkina Faso	5.93	27. Rwanda	4.62
7. Zambia	5.76	28. Togo	4.53
8. Malawi	5.66	29. Senegal	4.52
9. Afghanistan	5.43	30. Gabon	4.49
10. Angola	5.43	31. Central African Republic	4.46
11. South Sudan	5.43	32. Guinea-Bissau	4.30
12. Mozambique	5.27	33. Madagascar	4.28
13. Nigeria	5.25	34. Gaza Strip	4.24
14. Ethiopia	5.23	35. Eritrea	4.14
15. Timor-Leste	5.11	36. Yemen	4.09
16. Benin	5.04	37. Ghana	4.09
17. Tanzania	4.95	38. Western Sahara	4.07
18. Guinea	4.93		
19. Sierra Leone	4.83		
20. Cameroon	4.82		
21. Liberia	4.81		

---

1 CIA Fact Book at https://www.cia.gov/library/publications/the-world-factbook/rankorder/2127rank.html

39. Mauritania	4.07	74. Cambodia	2.66
40. Sudan	3.92	75. Israel	2.62
41. Gambia, The	3.85	76. Malaysia	2.58
42. Comoros	3.76	77. Kiribati	2.56
43. Cote d'Ivoire	3.63	78. Micronesia,	
44. Zimbabwe	3.56	Federated	
45. Kenya	3.54	States of	2.55
46. Iraq	3.41	79. Kuwait	2.53
47. Solomon Islands	3.36	80. Fiji	2.51
48. Tonga	3.36	81. India	2.51
49. Vanuatu	3.36	82. Djibouti	2.47
50. Papua New		83. Bangladesh	2.45
Guinea	3.24	84. Guam	2.38
51. Marshall Islands	3.22	85. Panama	2.38
52. Jordan	3.16	86. Faroe Islands	2.38
53. Philippines	3.06	87. Botswana	2.37
54. Tuvalu	3.03	88. Dominican	
55. Belize	3.02	Republic	2.36
56. Guatemala	2.99	89. United Arab	
57. American Samoa	2.98	Emirates	2.36
58. Samoa	2.94	90. Venezuela	2.35
59. Nauru	2.93	91. Kazakhstan	2.34
60. Laos	2.90	92. Cabo Verde	2.34
61. Swaziland	2.88	93. Nepal	2.30
62. Egypt	2.87	94. Ecuador	2.29
63. Pakistan	2.86	95. Mexico	2.29
64. Oman	2.86	96. Cook Islands	2.27
65. Honduras	2.86	97. Argentina	2.25
66. West Bank	2.83	98. Namibia	2.25
67. Bolivia	2.80	99. South Africa	2.23
68. Haiti	2.79	100. Mongolia	2.22
69. Algeria	2.78	101. Peru	2.22
70. Lesotho	2.78	102. Indonesia	2.18
71. Tajikistan	2.76	103. Burma	2.18
72. Kyrgyzstan	2.68	104. Saudi Arabia	2.17
73. Syria	2.68	105. Morocco	2.15

106. Guyana	2.14	140. United Kingdom	1.90
107. Sri Lanka	2.13	141. Seychelles	1.88
108. Turkmenistan	2.10	142. Sweden	1.88
109. Grenada	2.09	143. Iceland	1.88
110. Sint Maarten	2.09	144. Cayman Islands	1.86
111. Curacao	2.09	145. Norway	1.86
112. France	2.08	146. Iran	1.85
113. Turkey	2.08	147. Vietnam	1.85
114. Libya	2.07	148. Chile	1.84
115. Colombia	2.07	149. Uruguay	1.84
116. Greenland	2.06	150. Aruba	1.84
117. Dominica	2.05	151. Saint Vincent and	
118. Jamaica	2.05	the Grenadines	1.84
119. New Zealand	2.05	152. Brunei	1.82
120. Antigua and		153. Bahrain	1.81
Barbuda	2.03	154. Uzbekistan	1.80
121. Bhutan	2.02	155. Brazil	1.79
122. Northern Mariana		156. Saint Kitts	
Islands	2.01	and Nevis	1.78
123. United States	2.01	157. Netherlands	1.78
124. Suriname	2.01	158. Luxembourg	1.77
125. Ireland	2.00	159. Georgia	1.77
126. Tunisia	2.00	160. Mauritius	1.77
127. New Caledonia	1.99	161. Saint Lucia	1.77
128. Nicaragua	1.99	162, Australia	1.77
129. Korea, North	1.98	163. Wallis	
130. Bahamas, The	1.97	and Futuna	1.76
131. Paraguay	1.96	164. Maldives	1.76
132. French Polynesia	1.95	165. Virgin Island	1.75
133. Bermuda	1.95	166. Anguilla	1.75
134. El Salvador	1.95	167. Lebanon	1.74
135. Isle of Man	1.94	168. Denmark	1.73
136. Qatar	1.92	169. Finland	1.73
137. Gibraltar	1.92	170. Palau	1.71
138. Azerbaijan	1.91	171. Trinidad and	
139. Costa Rica	1.91	Tobago	1.71

172.	Turks and Caicos Islands	1.70	
173.	Liechtenstein	1.69	
174.	Barbados	1.68	
175.	Jersey	1.66	
176.	Belgium	1.65	
177.	Armenia	1.64	
178.	Puerto Rico	1.64	
179.	Russia	1.61	
180.	Macedonia	1.59	
181.	Canada	1.59	
182.	Saint Helena, Ascension, and Tristan da Cunha	1.58	
183.	Moldova	1.56	
184.	Saint Pierre and Miquelon	1.56	
185.	China	1.55	
186.	Guernsey	1.55	
187.	Malta	1.54	
188.	Switzerland	1.54	
189.	Portugal	1.52	
190.	Monaco	1.52	
191.	Albania	1.50	
192.	Thailand	1.50	
193.	San Marino	1.49	
194.	Spain	1.48	
195.	Belarus	1.47	
196.	Estonia	1.46	

197.	Cuba	1.46
198.	Cyprus	1.46
199.	Croatia	1.45
200.	Bulgaria	1.44
201.	Czech Republic	1.43
202.	Austria	1.43
203.	Germany	1.43
204.	Serbia	1.42
205.	Italy	1.42
206.	Hungary	1.42
207.	Greece	1.41
208.	Japan	1.40
209.	Slovakia	1.39
210.	Andorra	1.38
211.	Latvia	1.35
212.	Poland	1.33
213.	Slovenia	1.33
214.	Romania	1.32
215.	Ukraine	1.30
216.	Montserrat	1.29
217.	Lithuania	1.29
218.	Bosnia and Herzegovina	1.26
219.	British Virgin Islands	1.25
220.	Korea, South	1.25
221.	Hong Kong	1.17
222.	Taiwan	1.11
223.	Macau	0.93
224.	Singapore	0.80

Bibliography

Abelson, Raziel and Friquegnon, Marie Louise. *Ethics for Modern Life*, 6th ed. (New York: Bedford/St. Martin's, 2002).

Bonevac, Daniel. Today's *Moral Issues*, 3rd ed. (New York: McGraw-Hill, 1998).

Central Intelligence Agency. "Country Comparison: Total Fertility Rate [2014]" in *CIA World Factbook*; online at https://www.cia.gov/library/publications/the-world-factbook/rankorder/2127rank.html

Clark, John. "Capabilities Theory and the Limits of Liberal Justice. A Review Article on Martha Nussbaum's 'Frontiers of Justice'" in *Human Rights Review*, Volume 10, Issue 4 (2009), pp. 583–604.

Clark, John. "It Is What It Isn't! A Defense of Dialectic" *Review 31* (Jan. 5, 2014), online at http://review31.co.uk/essay/view/7/it-is-what-it-isn't-a-defence-of-the-dialectic.

Coffin, Tristram. "World Food Supply: The Damage Done by Cattle-Raising" in *The Washington Spectator*, vol. 19, no. 2 (Jan. 15, 1993).

Davis, Mike. *Late Victorian Holocausts: El Niño Famines and the Making of the Third World* (London and New York: Verso Books, 2002).

Davis, Mike. *Planet of Slums* (London and New York: Verso, 2007).

Di Leo, Jeffrey R. *Morality Matters: Race, Class, and Gender in Applied Ethics* (New York: McGraw-Hill, 2002).

Engelman, Robert. *More: Population, Nature, and What Women Want* (Washington, D.C.: Island Press, 2008).

Failkowski, Anthony. *Moral Philosophy for Modern Life* (New York: Prentice Hall, 1997).

Fund for Democratic Communities. "Ed Whitfield on why the 'teaching a man to fish' parable is a lie"; online at https://www.youtube.com/watch?v=fPcIumnhB8I.

Garrett Hardin Society. *Garrett Hardin Society Website*; online at http://www.garretthardinsociety.org/.

Gettleman, Jeffrey. "East Africa: The Most Corrupt Country," *New York Review of Books* Vol. LVII, No. 1 (Jan. 14, 2010).

Global Footprint Network. *Global Footprint Network Website*; online at http://www.footprintnetwork.org/. Government of Kerala. *Official Government of Kerala Website*; online at http://www.kerala.gov.in, updated on August 4, 2010.

Gregg, Alan. "A Medical Aspect of the Population Problem," in *Science*, 121, May 1955, pp. 681-682.

Hardin, Garrett. "Living on a Lifeboat" in *BioScience*, Vol. 24, No. 10, 1974, pp. 561-568; online at the *Garrett Hardin Society website* at: http://www.garretthardinsociety.org/articles/art_living_on_a_lifeboat.html.

Hardin, Garrett. "The Tragedy of the Commons" in *Science*, Vol. 162, No. 3859, December 13, 1968, pp. 1243-1248.

Hinman, Lawrence M. *Contemporary Moral Issues: Diversity and Consensus*, 2nd ed. (New York: Prentice Hall, 1999).

Ionesco, Eugene. *Rhinoceros and Other Plays* (New York: Grove Press, 1960).

Kinsley, Michael. "The Intellectual Free Lunch" in *The New Yorker*, February 6, 1995.

Kirk, G.S. and Raven, J.E. *The Presocratic Philosophers* (Cambridge: Cambridge University Press, 1969).

Koggel, Christine M. *Moral Issues in Global Perspective* (Peterborough, ON: Broadview Press, 1999).

Lappé, Francis Moore, Collins, Joseph, and Rosset, Peter. *World Hunger: Twelve Myths* (New York: Grove Press, 1998).

Lavietes, Stuart. "Garrett Hardin, 88, Ecologist Who Warned About Excesses" in *New York Times*, October 28, 2003; online at http://www.nytimes.com/2003/10/28/us/garrett-hardin-88-ecologist-who-warned-about-excesses.html.

Letablier, Marie-Thérèse. "Fertility and Family Policies in France," *Journal of Population and Social Security,* "Supplement to Volume one," online at: www.ipss. go.jp/webj-ad/Webjournal.files/population/2003_6/9. Letablier.pdf

Linebaugh, Peter. *The Magna Carta Manifesto: Liberties and Commons for All* (Berkeley and Los Angeles, 2008).

Mappes, Thomas and Zembaty, Jane. *Social Ethics: Morality and Social Policy* (New York: McGraw-Hill, 2006).

Marx, Karl. "Critique of the Gotha Program," in *Marx/ Engels Selected Works, vol. 3* (Progress Publishers: Moscow, 1970), pp. 11-30; online at https://www. marxists.org/archive/marx/works/1875/gotha/.

Marx, Karl. *Economic and Philosophical Manuscripts of 1844* (Moscow: Progress Publishers, 1974).

Marx. Karl. *The Eighteenth Brumaire of Louis Bonaparte* (Moscow: Progress Publishers, 1937); online at https:// www.marxists.org/archive/marx/works/download/ pdf/18th-Brumaire.pdf.

Maschke, Ed. "Tribute to Garrett Hardin: Making space in the lifeboat"; online at the *Garrett Hardin Society website* at: http://www.garretthardinsociety.org/ tributes/tr_maschke_2003sep.html.

May, Larry, Collins-Chobanian, Shari and Wong, Kai. *Applied Ethics: A Multicultural Approach* (New York: Prentice Hall, 2005).

Mies, Maria and Shiva, Vandana. *Ecofeminism* (London and Atlantic Highlands, NJ: Zed Books, 1993).

Mies, Maria. *Patriarchy and Accumulation on a World Scale: Women in the International Division of Labor* (London and New York: Zed Books, 1998), p. 117.

Murdoch, William W. Murdoch and Oaten, Allan. "Population and Food: Metaphors and the Reality" *Bioscience* 25, 1975.

Nagendra, Harini and Ostrom, Elinor. "Governing the commons in the new millennium: A diversity of institutions for natural resource management" in *Encyclopedia of Earth* (August 12, 2008); online at http://www.eoearth.org/article/Governing_the_commons_in_the_new_millennium%3A_A_diversity_of_institutions_for_natural_resource_management.

O'Hearn, Denis. "Amartya Sen's Development as Freedom: Ten Years Later" in *Policy & Practice: A Development Education Review*, Vol. 8, Spring, pp. 9-15; online at http://www.developmenteducationreview.com/issue8-focus1?page=show.

Olen, Jeffrey, Van Camp, Julie C. and Barry, Vincent. *Applying Ethics: A Text with Readings*, 8th ed. (Belmont, CA: Wadsworth Publishing, 2004).

Organisation for Economic Co-operation and Development. "Aid Flows Top USD 100 Billion in 2005," *OECD Website*, April 4, 2006; online at: http://www.oecd.org/document/40/0,2340,en_2649_33721_36418344_1_1_1_1,00.html.

Pimentel, David, et al, "Environmental and Economic Costs of Soil Erosion and Conservation Benefits," *Science*, Vol. 267, no. 5201, February 1995.

Pojman, Louis P. *Life and Death: A Reader in Moral Problems*, 2nd ed. (Belmont, CA: Wadsworth Publishing, 1999).

Pogge, Thomas. "'Assisting' the Global Poor" in Deen K. Chatterjee, ed., *The Ethics of Assistance: Morality and the Distant Needy* (Cambridge: Cambridge University Press, 2004).

Rand, Ayn. *The Fountainhead* (New York: Plume, 1994).

Reynolds, Terrence. *Ethical Issues: Western Philosophical and Religious Perspectives* (Belmont, CA: Wadsworth Publishing, 2005).

Roodman, David. An Index of Donor Performance, Center for Global Development, April 2004, online at http://www.globalissues.org/TradeRelated/Debt/USAid.asp.

Roy, Arundhati. *The Cost of Living* (New York: Modern Library, 1999).

Roy, Arundhati. "The Greater Common Good," *Friends of River Narmada Website*, April 1999; online at http://www.narmada.org/gcg/gcg.html.

Salleh, Ariel. *Ecofeminism as Politics: Nature, Marx and the Post Modern* (London and New York: Zed Books, 1997).

Salleh, Ariel. *Eco-Sufficiency & Global Justice: Women Write Political Ecology* (London and New York: Pluto Press, 2009).

Satris, Stephen. *Taking Sides: Clashing Views on Moral Issues*, 11th ed. (New York: McGraw-Hill/Dushkin, 2007).

Sen, Amartya. "Population: Delusion and Reality," in *New York Review of Books*, Vol. 41, No. 15, September, 22, 1994, pp. 62-71; online at: http://www.uwmc.uwc.edu/geography/malthus/sen_NYR.htm.

Starr, C. and Taggart, R. *Biology: The Unity and Diversity of Life*, 5th ed. (Belmont, CVA: Wadsworth Publishing Co., 1981).

Sharma, Devinder. "The Kalahandi Syndrome: Starvation in Spite of Plenty"; online at http://www.mindfully.org/Food/Kalahandi-SyndromeSharma19apr02.htm.

Shiva, Vandana. *Staying Alive: Women, Ecology and Development* (London and Atlantic Highlands, NJ: Zed Books, 1989).

Singer, Peter. "Famine, Affluence, and Morality" in *Philosophy and Public Affairs*, Vol. 1, No. 1, Spring 1972, pp. 229-243.

Sommers, Christina Hoff, and Sommers, Fred. *Vice and Virtue in Everyday Life: Introductory Readings in Ethics* (Belmont, CA: Wadsworth Publishing, 2003).

Sterba, James P. *Morality in Practice*, 5th ed. (Belmont, CA: Wadsworth Publishing, 1996).

Timmons, Mark. *Disputed Moral Issues: A Reader* (New York: Oxford University Press, 2006).

U.S. Bureau of the Census. *Statistical Abstract of the United States: 1974* (Washington, D.C.: U.S. Bureau of the Census, 1974).

U.S. Bureau of the Census. *Statistical Abstract of the United States: 1976* (Washington, D.C.: U.S. Bureau of the Census, 1976).

U.S. Bureau of the Census. *Statistical Abstract of the United States: 1979* (Washington, D.C.: U.S. Bureau of the Census, 1979).

U.S. Bureau of the Census. *Statistical Abstract of the United States: 1993* (Washington, D.C.: U.S. Bureau of the Census, 1993).

Van Wyk, Robert. "Perspectives on World Hunger and the Extent of our Positive Duties," *Public Affairs Quarterly,* Vol. 2, No. 2 (Apr., 1988), pp. 75-90

Vaughn, Louis. *Doing Ethics: Moral Reasoning and Contemporary Issues* (New York: W.W. Norton and Co., 2007).

Wackernagel. Mathis, et al, "Tracking the ecological overshoot of the human economy" in *Proceedings of the National Academy of Sciences of the United States of America [PNAS],* vol. 99 no. 14, pp. 9266–9271.

White, James E. *Contemporary Moral Problems* (Belmont, CA: Wadsworth Publishing, 2005).

About Changing Suns Press:

We are a volunteer-run, collective anti-authoritarian publishing project. We are committed to the production and dissemination of engaging political, Do-It-Yourself, fiction and scholarly publications. We publish both original manuscripts and translations.

Support Changing Suns Press:
Become a supporter of Changing Suns Press which will help in the production of our upcoming publications.

One Year Book Supporter
$300: Every book Changing Suns Press put out for a year from when you sign up plus 50% off all website purchases. We will also send you a CSP T-Shirt with your first shipment.

One Year E-Book Supporter
$150: Every ebook Changing Suns Press put out for a year from when you sign up plus 50% off e-book website purchases.

Contact us at:
Changing Suns Press
2138 McIntyre Street
Regina, SK
S4P 2R7
Canada
info@changingsunspress.com

Follow us at:
Twitter: @Changing_Suns
Facebook: https://www.facebook.com/changingsunspress/

Also Available from Changing Suns Press

Killing King Abacus
Anthology

a collection of writings for relations
without measure

**Killing King Abacus
Anthology**

ISBN: 978-0-9951551-0-7

6 x 9 | 308 pages

New introductions by
sasha k
Leila &
Wolfi Landstreicher

plus an anthology
introduction by
Chris Kortright

To Kill King Abacus is to create relations without measure. If we aim to destroy capitalism we cannot reproduce its necrophilic logic which reduces relationships to numbers. To Kill King Abacus is to destroy the social net which privileges mediated transactions and images over direct relations. Because money is a general equivalent and thus is nearly limitless in its applications, it conquers other signifiers of value; capitalism transforms other value systems into itself. To Kill King Abacus is to disrupt this process of quantification. Money may be the most indiscriminate of whores but capitalism is not the only system which measures value. Justice, morality, law and culture itself are all value systems which weigh, judge and channel human action. We want to create relations which defy such equations. We therefore have no need for standardizing models within our struggle. In the absence of value systems desire shoots in new directions. Insurrection is desire rebelling against value.

Also Available from Changing Suns Press

A Labour of Liberation by Baijayanta Mukhopadhyay

ISBN: 978-0-9951551-1-4
4.5 x 7 | 76 pages

This book explores the forms of labour—from the cognitive to the emotional, from the physical to the administrative—that go into contemporary healthcare, tracing the lineage of the hierarchies that have developed in alliance or complicity with state and capital.

Prase for *A Labour of Liberation*:
"In A Labour of Liberation, Baijayanta Mukhopadhyay offers a doctor's engagement with the tangled politics of healthcare today, struggling to imagine a care that does not perpetuate inequality and structural violence. It starts with recognizing that we are all healthcare workers, and that the tendency to think of medicine as technical reinforces privilege and ignorance. But then what? How deep would the change have to go? Based on an amazingly helpful bibliography of radical thought around healthy societies, the answer is far beyond what is comfortable for him, for us, for society. But we stay with the trouble. This is required reading for anyone in the healthcare industry and who thinks they are critical of it."

— Joseph Dumit author of *Drugs for Life: How Pharmaceutical Companies Define Our Health* and *Picturing Personhood: Brain Scans and Biomedical Identity*